looking at
BUSES

WHITE
Schweppes GINGER ALE
M
337

looking at BUSES

G.G.Hilditch

LONDON

IAN ALLAN LTD

Contents

First published 1979

ISBN 0 7110 0870 1

Published by Ian Allan Ltd, Shepperton, Surrey; and printed in the United Kingdom by Ian Allan Printing Ltd

MOSELEY AND
ACOCKS GREEN 1A
93
AEC
AHX 63

Author's Note

It occurred to me about ten years ago that whilst a good deal of literature existed that covered the history of the road passenger transport industry in general or of its various constituent members in particular, seldom if ever did one come across reading matter that dealt with the way in which buses (or trams) had performed in daily service, unless it was of such a highly technical nature as to be virtually uninteresting to the average lay enthusiast.

Consequently I spent one wet weekend writing a trial article largely for my own amusement, an article which was later accepted by the Editor of *Buses* and then published in the issue for May, 1968 under the pen name 'Gortonian'; a pseudonym that was adopted partially because I was initiated into the world of transport engineering in that suburb of Manchester and partially because my first subjects, the vehicles of the now defunct Crossley company, were natives of that same parish.

This trial article was followed by 17 more and at that stage the publisher suggested that a selection might be brought together into book form so as to provide a more permanent record. Perhaps this task has been undertaken at a most opportune time, for due to a combination of manufacturing mergers, changes in organisation within the industry and the impact of the Government's bus grant scheme, many passenger-carrying vehicles that only a few years ago seemed to have an assured future are now virtually obsolescent and must disappear in the very short term.

Consequently seven of the original articles have been revised and rearranged so as to provide an insight into the art of fleet engineering and then cover things old, things familiar, and things quite new in a proper chronological order. Two new sections have also been added, one dealing with the famous Bristol marque and the other with the author's brief encounter with tramway operation, a fascinating interlude in a trade which is now virtually extinct.

I trust in conclusion that the book will evoke as many happy memories for the reader as it did for me in the writing, and if dedication is neccessary then I would offer it to those men and women whose activities are so seldom appreciated by the travelling public and who —

'Labour to keep the wheels turning'

Acknowledgements

Over the years the author has been privileged to make the acquaintance of many senior executives of the road passenger transport industry and has been enabled as a result to refer in these pages to some of their experiences. Some of these gentlemen, alas, such as Mr A. G. Grundy of the SHMD Joint Board, Mr Harold Hattersley former Managing Director of Karrier Motors, Huddersfield, Mr Les Simpson late Chief Engineer East Yorkshire Motor Services, Mr G. Craven of Halifax Corporation, Mr Tom Bamford of Doncaster Corporation and M J. A. Abbott formerly General Manager of the Northern Counties Motor & Engineering Co, are no longer with us but I have many memories of the conversations that we had in the past and am grateful for the information that they provided.

Information about vehicles running in the late 1920s or early 1930s requires the possession of a very long memory if it is to be offered not only first-hand but also accurately and here numerous past colleagues, many of whom have now retired from office, have made substantial contributions. The questions that I put to them provided me with many leads but these often needed to be backed up by some detailed research, a process which was undoubtedly furthered by the way in which so many friends have had old records turned up for me or else have taken the trouble to extract photographs from their departmental files, tasks which are in no way connected with present day bus manufacturing or operating problems. Here I would especially thank Mr D. G. Houghton, Sales Director of Gardner Engines, Patricroft, Mr R. S. Crouch, previously Bus Sales Manager of the Daimler Company, Mr R. S. Boschell, Director and General Manager of Chas H. Roe Ltd, Mr T. R. Nicoll, formerly General Manager, Bristol Commercial Vehicles, Mr E. G. Foster, previously Director of Willowbrook Ltd, Mr J. W. Eaton who latterly held the position of General Service Manager, AEC Limited, Mr Brian Bancroft also formerly of the company, Mr G. F. Hughes of the old Tilling Stevens concern, together with other various assistants who have also been involved.

On the operating side, Mr R. Brook and Mr H. Tennant of the National Bus Co have been particularly helpful whilst Messrs Bardsley, Franklin, Davies, Rostron, Griffiths, Lord, Murray, Thompson, Thorpe, Taylor and Proctor, General Managers or former General Managers of the Swindon, Blackpool, Doncaster, Huddersfield, Rotherham, Leeds, Glasgow, Manchester, Newport, Oldham and Rochdale Municipal Undertakings also helped in this way.

Mr M. J. Tozer, an acknowledged expert on Bristol vehicles, also went to considerable trouble to provide information about that company's earlier activities. This leads me to the photographs used in these pages. It was my desire to use illustrations which had not been previously published in any transport book and I believe that this ambition has been largely realised and here Mr John Parke, Mr Alan Townsin and those other indefatigable photographers Mr R. F. Mack, Mr G. F. Mills and the late R. B. Parr opened their files to me. Mr Trevor Bray also made available some of the Karrier pictures taken by his father almost 50 years ago. Depot staffs often regard photographers as something of a nuisance but it is on occasions such as this that one has to be thankful that there are enthusiasts prepared to go to a great deal of trouble to provide a visual record of the industry's progress, something usually sadly neglected by those engaged within it. Unfortunately, I have been unable to ascertain who actually took some of the pictures but I would pay tribute to their anonymous efforts.

Finally, I am indebted to my former colleagues in a certain northern transport organisation who were subjected in the past to what can only be described as an engineering inquisition and who bore the experience with courtesy, patience and fortitude.

1 The Swinging Scene

Believe it or not but it is a fact people seldom appreciate that you cannot have a bus service without buses. How though do you come to acquire a double-decker? Certainly not from the used car lot down the road.

Actually the procedure is fairly complex, at least in so far as one of the larger vehicle-operating companies is concerned. It seemingly commences at a board meeting when the general manager puts forward his purchase recommendations, but actually things are then already some way along the road.

These recommendations will invariably have been the subject of some exchange of views between that official and his traffic and engineering executives who, sad to say, have often widely differing views as to what is the ideal form of vehicle. This difference though is not really to be wondered at, for the traffic side want to carry as many persons at one time as possible using the minimum amount of crewing, whilst the engineer knowing that he will be faced with the task of maintaining this contemplated rolling stock and having an inbuilt horror of complications, or gadgetry, wants, before anything else, simplicity plus tank-like construction.

Therefore, the purchase of a new batch of buses, like matrimony, has to be entered into with sobriety, discretion and extreme caution for, once obtained, they are likely to be around for a very long time as the average age at obsolescence now borders on the 15-year mark. In that period almost anything can happen, for traffic trends and hence vehicle requirements alter, manufacturers go out of production, (and sometimes spares go with them) or in extreme, and fortunately very rare, cases the chosen model just cannot do the work with which it is supposed to cope.

Before that recommendation ever reaches the board, however, certain other essential preliminaries have been undertaken, for having finally established the type and size which it is felt will best meet the concern's requirements, chassis and body specifications are drawn up, and despatched to as many manufacturers as management favours or can find.

Some manufacturer/operator discussions as to points of detail usually follow at this stage. Next come the tenders which invariably reproduce the specification modified as might be necessary, include a general arrangement drawing, and give in addition two other essential facts, namely price and suggested delivery period.

Price can give both the company accountant and the board a severe shock, (although the Grant scheme has done much to offset the worst effects) whilst delivery dates might provide even more all round heartburn. A prudent management in the present year of our Lord will order at least two years in advance and then count itself lucky if the target date is met. If not it becomes necessary to juggle the need to spend money on the recertification of old buses with works capacity and the extent to which fleet strength can be reduced and still not only provide a full service each night but also cope with those unforeseen emergencies which always rear their heads when buses are in short supply.

At last though the great day comes when a new bus is delivered and thereafter licensed, insured, certified, crewed (and we hope paid for) and goes out on its first service journey. But now comes the crunch, for service

Above right: Down in the depot — circa 1948. A nostalgic view taken in the Skircoat Road shops of Halifax Passenger Transport. In the foreground No208 has lost its 8.8litre engine. No302 on the left is one of the London RT type chassis which went into provincial service.

Right: Halifax again. A rare shot of a vanished prewar practice. The body of AEC single-decker No144 of 1934 is being removed prior to the chassis being given a complete overhaul.

44
17
JX 9402
MILL BANK
JX 327

RISHWORTH
54

means servicing, and without maintenance I wouldn't give that bus a fortnight on the road. Let us therefore digress here and take a light hearted look at a typical 24 hours in the life of a fleet engineer.

The day usually begins at around nine in the morning, provided of course that the preceding night has been uneventful, for one often has occasion to regret the inventive genius of the late Alexander Graham Bell, but if the worst has not happened, and you arrive fresh and dewy eyed, the bloom can soon be eliminated by a quick glance at the awaiting paper work, which can be classed under three headings, namely yesterday's, today's and tomorrow's.

Yesterday's will include reports from the garages, and workshops, night foremens, notes, staff statements, and the changeover and defect sheets covering the previous 24 hours workings. Some will arrive written in a copper plate hand, but the majority can easily be dog eared, well greased, and inscribed in a form of medieval Chinese that takes a bit of deciphering until one becomes familiar with the code. Perhaps the most interesting of all are those which emanate from the night staff, for they exist in what is almost another world.

Now any night foreman worth his salt waits until refuelling has finished, and then checks the pump sheet against his fleet list. The purpose of this exercise is two-fold. It establishes firstly that every bus has returned home, and secondly that each has been filled and thus cannot suffer the embarrasment of running out of jungle juice during its next turn of duty, but from time to time gaps appear. Then these members of the staff who like detective novels, can pit their wits in solving the case of the missing bus. Sometimes the absentee is safely tucked up at the back of the garage, or forgotten in a workshop, but sometimes it is neccessary to go out on safari around the town just in case the traffic department has left it on the bus park or behind the town hall, but occasionally there is still no trace. Well it could be that the private hire department has extended an already extended tour without reference, or perhaps some love lorn swain, tired of tramping home after bidding his girl good night, has borrowed it, but whatever the reason that bus has to be traced if it takes all night.

The tenor of a letter written by one who has been engaged on such a wild bus chase can well be imagined, truly they do make interesting reading.

The letters for the day always demand instant attention and, invariably having started at managerial level, contain difficult questions about costs. Maintenance budgets are usually studied with infinite care, so it is as well to prepare oneself as soon as possible after the periodic budgetary statements are issued so as to have all the answers ready. As a rule these statements have two columns, one which relates to the last financial year, and the other to the current 12 months, and thus any variations are easily highlighted. It only needs a change in wage rates, or two or three connecting rods to come through their crankcase sides to put up running expenses by alarming amounts, and then the inquisition begins.

Serious thought and composition are, though, only ideals to be dreamed about because this paper contemplation is bound to be sadly interrupted both by Mr Bell's mechanism, and by a string of departmental callers. It is a certainty here that few of the latter ever come bearing tales of joy, quite the reverse in fact.

Such doleful recitations as 'The washing machine at X has broken down,' or 'A wheel has come off, and run through the police station door,' — a midwinter howler this — 'The boiler plant at central works has

Right: 'A job for the experts'. Single-decker No30 in an awkward predicament. Fortunately recovery on this scale is an art seldom practised.

failed, and if it isn't put right in 10 minutes everyone is going home,' are some of the heartrending cries that this author has heard, but at least one can always console oneself with the thought that life is never dull, and after coping with these crises arrive at the point of making a start on paper pile number three.

Tomorrow's stuff cannot as a rule be dealt with on the spot, but must be referred elsewhere in the department for investigation, and possible report. Did bus No 99 really need four different gaskets in 100 miles? Well, records should have the answer. Did apprentice 'A' go to the technical college last week? That is one for the training officer, and could well have come from the administration side of the undertaking which is charged with the duty of filling up the training board claim forms, and they really are worth looking at. Eventually though that pile of paper is reduced to civilised proportions, and then comes the time for a change of occupation, for, from about 10.30am onwards outside callers begin to appear.

They may start with a previously arranged visit of some suppliers representative whose firms products are the subject of queries or complaints, and these in turn can range from bodywork that is showing signs of premature age, or even rain inside when it has stopped raining out, to the quality of the last consignment of night cleaners' wash leathers, or the unpleasant percentage of sulphur content in the fuel which came on Thursday week. These things are important, for the engineering department (traffic staffs wages costs excepting) spends more money than any other section of a passenger transport undertaking. Consequently an eighth of a penny a gallon on fuel oil over an order for half a million gallons is an item that cannot be ignored.

The other callers may include persons seeking employment, or those who virtually appear out of the blue, and the latter are always worth seeing at least once for one can never tell just what they may have to offer or tell you. The routine acquisition of stores is taken care of by the purchasing department, but it is the engineer who will decide if anything new is to be tried, provided of course that the price falls within the normally allowed limits. Here again the range of products offered by the manufacturing and supply industries is almost beyond belief, anything from staples for use in upholstery work to a do-it-yourself garage construction kit.

It will be appreciated that up to now the one thing that our subject has not done is any engineering, but with luck there is usually time to extend one's activities into this field before lunch, and the recommended drill is to take a walk around the workshops.

Here though arises a problem, for a smart office suit and bus garage are not compatible partners. If you doubt this statement consider the case of the engineer who strolled into the washing bay and began to pass between two coaches. Unknown to him on the offside of one of these was a cleaner who had been washing some well-greased rear wheels. He had a bucket roughly two-thirds full of very dirty water remaining at the end of the work, decided it was a pity to waste the fluid, and consequently threw it on to the rear corner panels, or rather that was where he meant to throw it. Sad to say the water and the engineer met as the latter came out from behind the vehicle and the encounter was sulphurous. There is not a lot of trouble of this type in the sepulchred calm of the paintshop even if one has to marvel at the way in which the staff can run black lines down the side of a 36-footer in no time at all and never finish up with the slightest suspicion of a waver, or to compare a weekend effort at home on say the bathroom wall to the considerable expanse of roof on the average double-decker. Some care is often necessary though for paintshop foremen as a race, bless them, are as touchy as hens with chickens particularly when varnishing is in process. 'When varnishing vanish' is a good motto to adopt, but from time to time a bit of urge is called for, as otherwise gold leaf all round and a superduper gloss will replace the reasonable commercial finish that is all that is required. In a way, however, one has to feel a little sympathy, for the paintshop has not had it good in that sense since the days of the trams.

Bodywork now is a different matter. There was a day when opening the very door enabled you to loose yourself in a cloud of dust as the circular saws bit into timber that would form pillars (nothing less than 4in square oak would suit one of my former mentors) or floor lagging, or even interior panelling, but that is all a thing of the past, thanks to metal frames, treadmaster, and plastics.

Come to think of it, bodyshops now have the air of a boiler factory and sometimes the sound as well, for nearly every panel is riveted into place, and according to the chief of our establishment even a modest single-decker can find holes for around 1,400 rivets. The growth of traffic on the roads plus the increase in the box dimensions of buses must have made the fortunes of the aluminium companies, for there are far more minor skirmishes out on the highway than there ever were in the days of yore, and if that is not enough just think about the rear-engined bus situation.

On a conventional vehicle the driver perched on top of the front axle, now he sits several feet in front of it, and that overhang can take a bit of getting used to. The net result is a succession of inside the wheelbase hook ups on innocent lampposts or other items of street furniture, and even if there is nothing vital under the panelling such scrapes can give a fleet a very untidy look in no time at all.

Perhaps though the two worst bodyshop sights are

bad crash victims and wilful damages. The latter invariably involve seating and the mentality of the offenders can hardly be imagined. We had buses on one route which would return home from time to time with the upholstery out, and the rubber filling removed, and not a trace of that material which had been crumbled away was ever found but at least here we had a shrewd idea as to the use to which it was being put. Just what value can be put on a razor or knife slash across a piece of best hide?

Accidental repairs can involve almost complete rebuilds, and on occasions leave one wondering.Take for example the case of the underfloor-engined single-decker which failed to stop when the vehicle in front, a skeletal semi-trailer did. The back of the trailer cut through the dash of the bus, bent the steering column right back and amazingly the driver escaped with hardly a scratch, but miracles did not end there. Both front windscreens of the large curved variety fell out of their frames, and landed with a crash on the deck of the trailer, then bounced up and down a few times, and eventually went back undamaged into their original situations. Front dashes in tramway days were knocked up out of a slab of armour plate, a material which on the earlier buses was superseded by black iron or aluminium, but now we use glass fibre, and

most workshops boast their own plastics division which can turn out all sorts of components from cash trays to mud wings, or even the large front radiator cowls. The good thing about these is that repairs can be carried out as a rule quite easily with a little more matting, and a cupful of solvent.

The next port of call might well be the unit's shop where engines, gearboxes, air brake valves, axles, and all the other mechanical bits and pieces which have been stripped off buses either as a result of some failure, or having completing their alloted span of mileage are dismantled, inspected, rebuilt with any necessary replacements, and finally tested before being returned to stores.

The unit shop is the place that carries out the most delicate fittings, but the introduction of precision tools in the works of the manufacturers has made the work rather easier than it used to be in some respects. For example it is no longer necessary to line bore bearings after fitting them in their crank case, and then bed the crank itself with a deal of careful scraping, but on the other hand the increasing use of air-powered equipment and more sophisticated types of gearbox has placed a greater emphasis on things that hardly mattered a decade ago, and the layout of the department will have had to have been changed in consequence.

This is where bus work differs from that carried out in the usual private car garage, for such an establishment will often content itself with fitting an exchange unit. The bus concern will adopt the same procedure initially, but will then have to recondition its own displaced parts as manufacturers rebuilt assemblies are invariably expensive and often in short supply. This thought brings one quite naturally into the stores department, and there could be a sorry story, awaiting the telling.

When I was an apprentice I always felt very resentful towards storekeepers. They always seemed to keep me standing at the counter for an age before scrutinising my indent with meticulous care obviously intending to reject it if they could. If they could not there was bound to be a further delay before the desired articles were handed over, and one couldn't help coming to the conclusion that they just hated to part with anything.

Having reached advanced years I still think that they like to keep things in stock, but now I have sympathy for I know why. It is so difficult to obtain replacements and there are often increases in the local temperature when, for example, it is found that the last lot of spring shackle pins (now out of stock and three

Left: 'Ready for anything'. Typical of many AEC Matadors is this example fitted with a deep vee plough, and judging from the climatic conditions it could soon be needed.

Above right: 'Well salted'. The effects of salt corrosion are clearly shown by this shot of a metal-framed machine. The chequer plate of aluminium panel has been removed from the inside of the wheel arch.

Right: 'Inside view'. The decay around the wheel cut out below the inserted chisel will mean that a new interior stress panel will be required.

Above: 'What no tushy pegs?' An interesting comparison of an old and new worm wheel. Worm drive axles will continue to work until the bronze wheel teeth are almost non-existent.

Left: 'Under repair'. All the running units have been removed from this underfloor-engined Leyland here undergoing a complete overhaul. Note the carrier jacks which make axle removal an easy matter.

buses waiting) took 13 weeks to arrive, but then only half were despatched, and some of those lost in transit.

I think everyone appreciates the need to export, but it is a pity that occasionally some people who should not need reminding so to do, do not contemplate the needs of those at home who have to keep the wheels of vehicles around 10 years old, or occasionally alas a good deal younger than that, turning.

This is where though the 'Old Pals Act,' and that handy *Buses* magazine feature entitled Fleet news comes in. You read the column carefully each month and note and inwardly digest all you have seen. Two weeks later in comes a Crossley Venturer three-axle double-decker with chronic indigestion in the fuel system, no parts in stock, but delivery promised in three weeks. Next question . . . Who has any anywhere like it? Ah yes, the Rainbow Bus Company took three out of use last month, and you know Alf, the chief engineer. This is one of the fascinations of the business, because although the industry is nationwide almost everyone in it knows everyone else, so you give him a ring, chat over the state of life generally and borrow, without making a further mountain of paper until you can pay him back. It really is amazing to think of all the little packets of urgently-wanted spares that are dashing around the countryside in the boots of express buses, but what if Alf cannot help?

It may just be that a comment has been passed on the disposal aspect, so you ring the scrapyard, and the man there says 'Yes come and get it,' and here life has another treat in store. Scrap men are very necessary, always in a hurry, and often unconventional in both outlook and method. There was the occasion when we wanted an obsolete engine, and found one at the back of such an establishment stood upright in about four inches of oozing mud. The proprietor patted its flanks, and asked if we would care to hear it running. We in all innocence, and wet socks, nodded, when a bellow went up for one of his minions. That seven-feet-high and eight-feet-wide worthy appeared seconds later ploughing through the mud like a first war tank with a battery trolley in tow, and he duly hitched up the leads to the very dubious-looking starter. A can full of fuel was coupled to the fuel pump, and our hero then draped himself over the engine and hugged it to his breast. His boss flicked the trolley switch, the engine started to turn, then coughed, and then wonders of wonders roared into life. ROARED is the right word too, for it did not have any exhaust pipe or silencer and so to this accompaniment as Muscle Man held it down we bartered in sign language, until dazed and rather shattered we parted with £10. This episode occurred some years ago, and we no longer have that engine but it deserves an epitaph for it was still chugging happily on when we last had news of its existence.

I have seen occasions too when having wanted a gearbox, we have had to spin down the road from such a yard on trade plates, in some old timer, found the unit acceptable, and seen it and the engine cut out of the chassis with a blow torch whilst we waited. As I said scrapyards have their merits.

Oft times though you pass into the heavy repair shop still on your rounds and tend to think that you have a scrapyard all of your own on your hands. Such places have usually two sorts of operatives, namely stayers and runners going about their allotted tasks, but, despite the incredible number of standing buses, if the foreman is leaning against his desk puffing out rings from a pipe that contravenes the Smoke Abatement Act all is well; if he is absent from this well-worn post it is trouble, with a capital T.

The stayers are the men whose work stays with them for a reasonable period. They are most likely taking care of the heavy docking work, complete chassis overhauls, and big accident jobs, and once they get their teeth into a bus bits fly off in all directions, so by the time engine, gearbox, axles, radiator, springs, shackles, valves, and every possible piece of piping have been removed you can be forgiven for wondering if it will ever go again, but it does, and the satisfied smile on the face of the area mechanical engineer as he issues a further certificate of fitness after the overhaul has been completed makes the whole process well worthwhile.

The runners have a rather different life, for they are doing the intermediate jobs, too big for the garages, but not sufficient to ground a vehicle for overhaul. A good running fitter can not only tackle virtually anything but also translate the drivers' daily report sheets, and then quickly diagnose the faults. This is really the art of the job. You can have a bus sent in with a peculiar transmission whine. Anyone can hear it when the vehicle is in motion but locating the actual source, from a combination of engine, road, and body noises can be a very difficult thing to accomplish. Some tasks involve the most minor amount of final rectification, but a tremendous amount of discovery, and a good example is a leak in a vacuum pipe. It may not be possible to hear the hiss of the ingoing air, and the failure could be cause by the pipe chaffing under a clip in some remote situation, beneath the cab floor so then when it is found there follows the trouble of loosening the unions, uncleating the pipe itself and then performing a sort of snake charming act both to remove and restore it after the offending fault has been brazed up.

By this time lunch will be awaiting, provided that the canteen gas has not failed, or the water gone off. Most garages are now quite elderly, and as the run of the mains was either never charted or the charts were thrown out for salvage in 1916 the location of the

Above: 'Steady hands'. Lining is not a task to be undertaken on the morning after a night before, but a skilled man can maintain both a high speed and straight edges.

supplies is a mystery held deep in the memories of the maintenance section. You keep your fingers crossed here but if food does actually arrive, then its consumption can proceed simultaneously with the process of digesting the contents of the technical press, or other like literature, for one never seems to be able to spend sufficient time to assimilate all that is going on elsewhere.

Afternoons are a repetition of the morning with a return to callers or paper work, and might include one of those joyous occasions when staff and managerial representatives meet to discuss matters of topical importance over a pint of tea but if at all possible such proceedings are encouraged to end before about four of the clock for this is the daily instant of truth time.

If your engineer has a benevolent management he should have a blessed vehicle surplus available of 15 per cent over maximum peak hour output. On the face of things, 40 extras on a fleet of say 270 looks to be a very comfortable margin but... have say five on heavy overhaul, three in the bodyshop, and three in the paintshop, and there goes 10. Take off one or two awaiting relicensing or entry to the works, the odd accident damage, a few gaskets blown, the one with a broken front spring, those undergoing the usual mileage dock, and the 10 becomes 20. It is at this state of the game that you hear that three drivers have just rung their steeds in with faulty brakes and that the school party that was on a morning visit to Vladivostock, and whose vehicles had been promised back by 15.00 hours at the latest 'certain' has been delayed because they have lost young Johnny, so before you can say 'Guy,' there is a shortage. Shortages can vary from depot to depot, and then that device of Mr Bell does become useful, for a spot of lease-lend can be arranged provided of course that a highbridge decker does not stray to a severely restricted single-deck route, or you are not trying to prize away some superintendent's best bus that he is carefully nursing for a rainy day.

This last part of the normal working day can be hectic, with an anxious secretary hovering around to ensure that if nothing else the mail goes out on time, but at last the depots are empty, the workshops closed, and peace reigns . . . for about ten minutes.

If anything has to go wrong it will happen in the middle of the evening peak, or if a crisis is evaded by some good fortune it may follow that a key pump man fails to appear to catch the buses as they roll back to the depot doors, and in no time at all the queue spills out on to the highway, thus offending the constabulary, who put in a formal, and quite unwanted appearance.

Even when goodwill is restored all round the day still has its moments, for choose to travel home by bus and anything can occur from a breakdown to the driver showing those on board how to drive a double-decker BRM style when gentle recriminations are the order of the day, and still the evening awaits, all ready to be filled in.

It could give the chance to try out some demonstrator, or to attend the meeting of one of the technical societies, or to visit a garage in order to see some member of the staff or a piece of suspect plant, or there could just be a happening, like the time when at 21.20 hours . . .

A double-decker all of 8ft wide rounded a bend on a rural road, or rather it started to round the bend. It never quite finished and instead followed a straight path, through a stone wall and down a 3ft drop, coming finally to rest in the midst of a herd of cows which rather remarkably did not resent the presence of this stranger in their grazing ground. The wrecking crew duly arrived, and gazed at the remarkable phenomenon of their subject standing naturally in the quiet of a summer evening on all four wheels amongst its bovine companions on their four legs; but the benevolence of the latter did not extend to our gang who spent the next half hour in the nearest thing to a rodeo that this side of the wild west has ever seen.

Eventually after pacifying both the animals and the farmer (he was the most difficult) attention could be given to the bus, but there was a snag. It could not he hauled up to road level without sustaining a great deal of damage, and the only other way out was via the fields and farm yard. The width of the latter was below 8ft, and the gate posts of millstone grit had been sunk down in the stoneage, but up they had to come, and the moon was riding high before that bus was once more on its way home. By that time the chap who put it into difficulties was no doubt tucked up in bed and dreaming as to what would be the best story to tell, on the morrow when high authority would be inviting his explanations.

Recovery work does not as a rule take place under ideal conditions, and it is therefore easy to guess why engineers hate the onset of winter, although things are much better now that most of the highway authorities possess a posse of highly-efficient salting or gritting machines. Twenty years ago though most of the few heavy recovery vehicles that existed were in the hands of the bus operators and so they had to become experts in snow clearance and road opening as well.

One concern was so affected by conditions during the infamous winter of 1946/7 that a number of ex-WD four-wheel drive vehicles was then purchased and during the following summer a variety of ploughing equipment was designed and made up. This included a vee plough about 4ft high and 8ft wide across the outer ends of the blades.

Those responsible actually prayed for snow thereafter and eventually it came, when on went the plough plus a set of wheel chains and out went the gang cheerfully ensconced in the cab which contained, amongst other home comforts, a heater, a piece of carpet, a small cooking stove, and various tins of soup taken from a wellknown range of 57 varieties.

Some way out of the town centre was a narrow road which ran between two high dry stone walls on a north-to-south axis, and a sharp east wind had lifted snow off the fields to windwards and deposited it inside the walls in drifts of around 3ft deep. The half-hourly bus service which used it promptly stopped — so here was an ideal place to try the new toy. Four-wheel drive was engaged, the plough dropped on to the skids, the driver yelled 'Geronimo' and charged full tilt into the obstructions. The spectacle was most satisfying. The snow flew in all directions as the machine ground its way forwards until it was brought to a halt, but then only a short reversal backwards was necessary when another charge could follow and further progress be recorded. In no time at all that road was cleared but retribution was to follow for the plough had in sweeping the snow sideways exerted a tremendous pressure on the walls which, not having mortared joints, collapsed outwards under the strain, and so yet another irate farmer had to be diplomatically dealt with, only this time it was the gneral manager who received the full onslaught making life a little difficult for all concerned thereafter.

It really is surprising just where buses can get to once they run out of road, but not every outing for the wrecking crews involves vehicle recovery. Sometimes new ground has to be broken and once again that aptitude to be able to cope with anything becomes of paramount importance.

One balmy summer eve the traffic department entered into a state of chaos, when a roadside building which was in the course of being steadily demolished decided to commit hari-kiri and largely collapsed. I say largely because the whole of a front wall remained standing and as this was some four stories high the police closed the highway to all traffic, which was unfortunate as at least eight services, four of which were main trunk routes, were thus affected.

The sooner that wall came down the sooner the buses could restart and, as time is money, out went the breakdown gang to try its hands as demolition experts.

On arrival at the scene the usual reconnaissance took place when one brave shinned up a ladder and fixed a stout chain around a third floor window frame. The tractor winch rope was then run out and affixed to the chain via a strong steel shackle and pin, the climber came down to earth, everyone stood back and torque was applied to the winch drum.

The assembled multitude — and the driver — expected the wall which was swaying in the breeze to come down but instead a moment of pure comedy ensued when instead the tractor went UP, like a spider on its thread.

Yet another consultation took place after restoration to terra firma and the services of a second similar machine consequently brought into play. This was run at right angles to and across the front of the first and both were harnessed together. Thus anchored a second pull was cautiously tried, the wall began to tilt, and was just reaching the critical point when a loud twang announced the parting of the shackle and the chain . . . which has never been seen since . . . took off in a southerly direction.

Below: 'Bench testing'. A Bristol AWV power unit on the test bed. The temporary exhaust, water, and recording connections are clearly visible.

Everyone present with self-preservation in mind simultaneously ducked and stepped back, not that they had anything to fear from the chain as it was heading for the stratosphere but there was another hazard. What a pity all this took place on the banks of a long disused and rather sludgy canal!

Here one comes to the aspect of self-control which all engineers learn sooner or later but the lesson can be painful. One engineer, who shall be nameless, was on his rounds one morning when he came across a double-deck casualty which had had the objuracy to fail with a broken front spring at the main door of the depot and, as broken plates had jammed up against the drag link, recovery was impossible until steering had been restored once more.

He 'gaffer like' watched the activities of the man on the job for a few moments and then being dissatisfied with progress told that worthy to insert a long bar in the indicated position and press downwards on the end whilst our friend pushed the broken bits into line. Thereafter he assumed a kneeling position by the front offside wheel . . . a most dangerous situation . . . and started to do his stuff when the bar slipped, the spring shot up once more and this time not only trapped the drag link but three fingers as well.

His assistant panicked and was doing nothing to free the sufferer whose language was turning rather ripe, when from the safety of the opposite pavement shambled a nondescript character who gazed down upon our anguishing hero and inquired 'Are you Mr X?'

On receiving the assurance that such was the case the newcomer then posed the all important question 'Please have you any vacancies for night cleaners?"

As my informant said, when you can give a polite answer to a question like that whilst your fingers are being efficiently flattened you know you have finally arrived, and truly it is the ability to cope in tricky situations that is the art of the job.

Engineering, though, basically involves vehicles and so let us turn now to the study of some of the more famous models that have provided, or are still providing, efficient and reliable passenger transport services. But before we do let me make a brief reference to those tender documents I mentioned on the first page. They usually come neatly contained in a semi-permanent folder and so being easy to store have a happy facility for finding their way into the archives, from whence they can be resurrected years afterwards by researchers such as this scribe and so provide a source of supply for many of the details that follow hereafter.

2 The Tinkling Tillings

I have never been quite able to decide exactly what first aroused my interest in transport generally, for there is here something of a 'chicken and egg' situation as I recall later in this manuscript. I was certainly attracted by a particular tram car but simultaneously I was experiencing the effects of a propaganda campaign that was then being waged by the lately lamented North Western Road Car Company.

That concern was rapidly expanding. It had, for example, only 51 vehicles at 21 January 1923 but by 31 December 1929 the fleet strength was up to 298, and in the meantime one innovation had been a new bus route which had obligingly passed our front garden gate. The arrival of the buses formed a topic of conversation amongst the adults in the family for weeks after the event. It is not surprising therefore, that any junior mind like mine was impressed, but then no one who had been brought up in this age when the possession of some private means of mechanical transport is commonplace, can appreciate just what a difference those red and white vehicles made to the life of everyone who was living in our village.

No longer did a shopping trip to the nearest township involve a long walk to the station, the catching of a rather infrequent train, and then another walk up a rather steep hill, with all that this meant when the day was wet or the shopping load heavy as was invariably the case. Now we had a bus every hour, and all that was necessary was to listen for its approach and then saunter out through the gate to meet it.

Picking up the noise that heralded an arrival was no problem. There was then, of course, little traffic apart from an odd lorry going to the local printing works, or the doctor's Morris coupe, but their signature tunes were pitched in a very different key from those of the engines which propelled the Tilling Stevens along, for of such make were these impressive buses. They did

Below: An early North Western petrol-electric circa 1925 with high chassis and a peculiar form of part solid, part roll top roof. Fleet numbers ran from 158-188.

not roar or wheeze or clatter, they simply tinkled, irrespective of whether they had one deck or two.

The latter fortunately did not pass often, which was just as well for two very sufficient reasons. Firstly their advance was marked by a steady rattling among the mantelpiece-mounted ornaments, and secondly the vibration and ride characteristics were such that even one mile of personal travel was enough to bring on all the symptoms of galloping travel sickness.

Numbered from 165 to 188 they dated from 1925 and were notable through the possession of solid tyres, high radiators, petrol electric transmission, and Brush 51-seat open-topped bodies. We only had them at holiday times when their extra capacity would be brought into play to deal with the crowds of hikers en route to or from the Peak District, most of whom no doubt relished the view they obtained from the top deck seats. But I for my part preferred the single-deck specimens and these consisted either of the 75 petrol-electrics in the range 100 to 204 whose delivery first commenced in 1924, or the later types B9 or B10 which had conventional transmission and began with No209 of 1927.

The petrol-electrics did not have a long life, being withdrawn by 1932, but the B10s as we shall see were in another class. They were in fact one of the aristocrats of the motorbus world, and as over 2,000 had been sold by 1929 as B10Bs with normal control or B10As with the more popular half-cab agreement they are worthy of a detailed description.

Prominent at the front end was a small radiator with its bowed centre strips and beside it, sticking out from the front of the dash plate, would be the business end of the bulb horn. Inside the cab at the rear of the said plate was stark simplicity. A steering wheel and column, the latter carrying a large ignition lever, an oil indicator, a gearchange lever hard up against the cab side sheet, the handbrake lever also on the lefthand side right beside it, two big slots in the floor and two pedals issueing there through, and, last but not least, the ignition switch, comprised all the control equipment with which the driver had to contend.

One other basic ingredient ....the starting handle... passed through the radiator and once this had been 'twissled', in local parlance, a few times the tinkling would begin.

It issued from the 5.12 litre four-cylinder side-valve petrol engine which could with an all-out effort produce 63.5bhp at 1,500rpm and here one could be excused for querying the appellation 'Express' that the factory had bestowed upon this amazing vehicle which as one wellknown technical writer of the day said 'has been designed with a policy of elimination in mind' — I would that buses in this present year of grace had.

The engine had an aluminium crankcase, two

Below: By 1928 orthodox transmission had been adopted. No227 was one of 66 vehicles new that year to North Western with Tilling 36-seat or Brush 32-seat bodies. 227 was a Tilling 36-seater.

Right: Tilling-Stevens built a number of three-axle petrol-electric double-deck chassis. This view of an example supplied in 1928 to Wolverhampton shows the locations of the engine-connected generator and propeller-shaft coupled motor.

Below right: 1929 saw the arrival of slightly raked windscreens, but despite its more modern look No333 still lacked the advantages offered by front wheel brakes.

separate twin cylinder blocks, a Zenith water-heated vertical carburettor, and a high tension magneto, which was carried across the front of the cylinders, and driven in tenadem with the water pump through the medium of a rather unusual right-angle drive.

You could if you wished to indulge in luxuries have electric lighting when the necessary dynamo might be powered from the timing gear, but that course was not recommended, and so most fittings of this type were mounted on the near-side frame member, just in front of the gearbox, and driven by a long flat leather belt. Here the dynamo benefited from the fresh air, and the belt from road dirt, grit and splash.

Behind the engine was an open clutch with a single plate and behind this again the four-speed remote-mounted crash gearbox into which ran three open selector rods. These coming from the gate at the bottom of the gear lever, were again of delightfully simple construction, and were lubricated 'as and when' by ye olde oil can, as indeed was the equally exposed clutch withdrawal mechanism, but not, I hasten to add, the withdrawal bearing. This item had to be removed at about 12,000-mile intervals, and then packed with grease.

I should think though that that job must have taken about 10 minutes.

An open propeller shaft complete with Hardy Spicer joints took the torque to the rear axle and here was a substantial underslung worm that must never have been overworked. There is not much doubt that this happy state of affairs did not apply to the two 14½in diameter × 2½in wide rear brake shoes, for although front brakes or a servo for that matter could be had by 1929 on very special request, all the standard chassis came out with the simple system so beloved of old, about which one could truthfully say that retardation

Above: North Western No557 was new in 1931. It formed a part of the 516-577 batch all of which had Brush 33-seat bodies.

Above right: A prewar TSM single-decker exemplified by this model delivered to Lucas & Son, Stockingford (Royal Purple), in 1932.

Right: This prewar double-decker of Mansfield District dates from 1931. It passed later to Midland General, another of the Balfour Beatty group of companies.

power was proportional to the strength of the driver's right foot — and produce a graph to prove it. Until 1931 that is, when numbers 516 to 521 appeared with these improvements.

Simplicity continued in that other important department, the steering system. The swivel pins were bushed... no bearings or thrust buttons here, nor were the track rod ends screwed for ease of adjustment. If the track was out the method used was to heat up the road... and bend it a bit to suit... but if this all seems a bit primitive remember that this was the AEC Regent of the 1920s. It was in fact an operator's bus and it did not need a lot of time consuming or fancy maintenance to keep it going.

And go it did! Sixty-three horsepower was by no means lavish even in 1929 for a forward control 16ft wheelbase full size 32-seater and particularly so in a region such as that of the Peak which abounds with steep gradients, but those Tillings tinkled along on a petrol consumption of about 8 to 9mpg and as for lubricating oil, well 500mpg was reasonable and 1,000mph rather more than commonplace.

The engine was truly a fantastic effort. There was so little to it, and it was so well thought out. If, for example, the tappets wanted adjusting all the mechanic had to do was to lift off the bonnet side, remove the tappet covers and then unscrew either the sparking plugs or the brassplugs fixed in the heads over the inlet valves, when the job could be completed without him hardly having to bend his back. Even if that engine was solidly bolted in the chassis frame what did it matter for the resulting vibration was scarcely noticeable.

The chassis prices in standard trim were £835 for the normal control version or £865 for the forward control model and in the case of the latter one received 57cwt of basic engineering for the outlay, so no wonder they proved to be very popular.

Body styling and equipment of course differed with whims of their owners, but those of the North Western company were quite comfortable to ride in over short distances and some possessed the extra refinement of a heating system. This consisted of two copper tubes plus a brass control valve fixed at the near side of the front bulkhead on the cantrail. Operation of the lever allowed fluid from the radiator to pass around the pipe somewhat in the manner of circa 'Prime of Miss Jean Brodie' low pressure water school heating system, and the end result was just about as efficient, but if this bit of bus was not just as good as perhaps it could have

NUNEATON

MANSFIELD
MANSFIELD
MANSFIELD

A rebuild, No521, was given a 1935 secondhand body in 1939. It survived with North Western until 1949 when it was sold to Crosville. Pictured in Macclesfield Bus Station.

been, the remainder was an engineering marvel. In fact in complete contrast to the Karriers of chapter IV I can only ever remember being let down by Tilling Stevens on one day, but what a day that was!

By some chance or other quite a number of people from our village in the Pennines — for by this time we had moved to the other end of North Western territory — had elected to take their annual holidays at the same resort, and this meant we should all be endeavouring to pick up the same east coast-bound bus at the same time. We had had some difficulties in obtaining accommodation previously so my father paid a visit to the local office of the company, and arranged for a duplicate to be provided which would start from our boarding place, and be reserved for the passengers he then booked.

The Saturday morning dawned clear and bright as we filled the valley bus and headed for the main road township where our long-distance steed should be waiting, only it was not, and it failed to arrive in the hour that we spent by the roadside after our scheduled departure time. Father rang up the area office, to be told that no one there had any knowledge of us but eventually it was admitted that an omission had been made and transport was being obtained from the nearest depot, so would we please wait.

We had no option, but at last I pricked up my ears as I heard that familiar tinkling sound, and then round the corner chugged our special. I suppose that finding a bus to run to Newcastle on a peak summer Saturday morning in 1938 was never easy, but the one we had been allocated was not even a rebuild. It was perhaps the oldest then remaining in original condition, but in we all piled, and with cases stacked in the gangway endeavoured to make ourselves as comfortable as possible.

I was looking forward to some tram spotting from my seat at the front but in no time at all my view was obliterated for we had a boil up, and as the cloud of steam increased so did speed decrease. We edged our way up to the top of Standedge, and just as slowly descended the Yorkshire side to Marsden where the driver, who was obviously hot in more places than just under the collar, rang for a changeover. He tried again at Huddersfield, and again at Dewsbury and then on reaching Leeds flatly refused to take the bus another yard.

The West Yorkshire company did its best but it was too busy so the replacement turned out to be another Tilling that had all the vintage look about it of the bus we had just quitted. It had some of the vice too, for once on the Great North Road beyond Ripon, the engine began to misfire and finally gave up the ghost altogether at Leeming Bar. We sat yet again by the roadside until in the late afternoon Tilling number three came on the scene, and apart from a little autovac problem at Durham took us to our ultimate destination without any further trouble.

It was sorry long distance story, but obviously very much of an exception for one company actually chose to retain its Tillings for long-distance work when it could, had it wished, have operated such flyers as Gilfords instead.

This concern was the predecessor of the now famous Yelloway company of Rochdale which although it then used the Yelloway fleetname actually traded as Holt Brothers of Rochdale, and possessed by 1930 a fleet of about 40 passenger vehicles made up of five rebodied Dennis' that had started life as charabancs, 10 Tillings (three with Massey bodies seven with Warwick coachwork), 10 Gilfords, and no less than 24 Reos of varying size and age.

These were utilised on the various services including that most fascinating one which, since 1928, has connected Rochdale with Torquay and at this time was running southwards on four days per week ie both days prior to the Easter 1931 holidays the company Saturdays, Sundays and Wednesdays with corresponding northward returns. Unfortunately, however, despite this and other commendable pioneering ventures the company fell on hard times and finally passed into bankruptcy in 1930. Operations though never quite came to an end although some routes were abandoned, and only a few days prior to the Easter, 1931 holidays the company was reformed under its present title, but further retrenchment was necessary, and so the fleet had to be reduced.

When one bears in mind the 300 miles which separates the two terminals of the Devon route and the journey time of 12hr then involved, the fact that Tillings here continued en bloc is a tremendous testimonial to their seldom-failing reliability, and rumour has it, surprising though it may seem that their ability to maintain a good average speed had a part to play here. In fact one bus-bodied version is to this day attributed with a London/Rochdale timing of under 4½hr, but not every trip was accomplished in such a time as I discovered through a first hand contact.

I was in the Torquay bus station one Saturday evening waiting for the arrival of a friend off the same Yelloway service, and came into conversation with one of the supervisors who in his earliest days had been involved with the Tillings.

He then told me of the occasion when he set out from Rochdale on Friday night, and drove through the dark hours to arrive in Devon early on the Saturday. Traffic was heavy, and as a number of passengers was still awaiting transport when all available scheduled buses had been loaded, he was asked if he would do the necessary, instead of going to his awaiting digs.

He agreed, and so after a wash and a meal started

the homewards run only in view of his previous activities this was regarded as a 'short working' being intended for Manchester only. Well! Late that Saturday evening the East Street station was reached, but his day was not yet done for an SOS had just been received from Blackpool where extra buses were urgently wanted, and so he set off for the Lancashire resort, on the understanding that a relief driver was made available at Preston and only there, when he had well over five hundred continuous miles to his credit, did he finally foresake the cab. During the whole of this time his machine had run like clockwork.

Despite the foregoing recommendation, however, the Tilling Stevens company recognised around 1930 that the pedestrian ways of the B10 series of vehicles were not going to be adequate in the future, and so plans were laid for the production of an improved machine, which could compete with the Regal or the Tiger, but not before certain Express chassis had acquired such startling innovations as Salerni semi-automatic transmission or Gardner 4L2 oil engines.

The newcomer appeared in 1931 after two years of deverlopment, and featured a six-cylinder petrol engine, which was given the type reference B60, and had two rather unusual features. The bore of 4in and the stroke of 5½in gave a swept volume of 414.7cu in or 6.972cc. This in terms of the even then outdated RAC formula spelt 38.4hp but in actual fact around 109bhp was produced at 2,500rpm. The head design was undertaken by Mr (as he then was) Ricardo himself, but here we come to the first unusual aspect, as each of the castings only covered two bores in marked contrast to the Leyland or AEC method of having one long head that ran the full length of the engine. The Tilling scored here but conversely item two was not so praiseworthy as only four main bearings were employed when most other manufacturers used seven.

The 17ft wheelbase chassis was completely new also, and the general appearance was certainly improved by the neat but very imposing polished aluminium radiator, which could be provided with thermostatically operated radiator shutters if the customer so required. Across the front of the radiator ran a substantial bar, and this carried two large dipping headlights, only the dipping was done not by utilising twin filament bulbs, but by solenoids which varied the position of the reflectors in the lamp housings, a now almost forgotten piece of automobile engineering practice.

The singleplate clutch was of the open type as employed on the B10 but the friction surfaces comprised two loose Ferodo rings, that were NOT fixed to either the driving or driven plates. This piece of unconventionality was adopted in the interests of maintenance for when they wore down to replacement limits the load could be taken off the nine pressure springs, and the rings, being floating, simply slipped out or in, but, alas, the idea whilst good in theory was none too successful in practice.

The gearbox continued to have four sets of forward ratios, was remotely mounted and possessed the outside selector shaft arrangement of the B10 but was insulated from the chassis by having Silentbloc mountings. The output was then taken via a normal type propeller shaft with Hardy Spicer joints to an underslung worm rear axle of ample proportions, which followed the fully floating principle.

Each of the rear hubs carried two brake shoes lying side by side, and these were covered by sizeable cast iron drums, but this material was not employed on the front axle, for although the machine now had both a vacuum servo, and front braking mechanism, the drums in which the front friction linings worked were steel pressings, flanged at the open ends, and surrounded by shrunk on rings to counteract any distortion tendencies.

The chassis was quite modern by 1931 standards, and possessed a very similar stablemate which had a wheelbase of 13ft 4½in and was designed to carry 56-seat double-deck bodywork. The first such example was given Beadle coachwork, and after registration as KJ 2915 was utilised for demonstration work.

Both were neat and well-sprung but included various antiquated features as standard such as a starter motor operating lever that sprouted from the front cab dash, the centre accelerator, and the retention of a gatechange gear lever, but nevertheless they represented a considerable advance on what had gone before. As the single-decker had a basic price of £1,075. (A Leyland Tiger TS1 was also £1,075, a Bristol Light Six £1,050, or the Daimler CH6 £1,250), it could be expected that sales would be considerable but this was never the case, although it did much better than the double-decker which virtually flopped, although Walsall, Birmingham, Portsmouth municipalities and Westcliff-on-Sea Motor Services were numbered among the few purchasers. It only needed a glance at the front of the radiator to see the reason why.

Previous vehicles to come out of the Maidstone works had carried the legend Tilling Stevens in full, but now the radiator badge was abbreviated to the initials TSM for Tilling was Tilling no longer. That organisation had severed its connection, and the now-reconstituted company had adopted the new style which it was to retain until 1937, when the old format reappeared once more, not that it made a lot of difference, for once the link with the constituent operating subsidiaries had gone, orders for the Maidstone-built vehicles began to taper off, and finally disappeared altogether. Although by absorbing the

Vulcan concern in 1937 and transferring all manufacture from Southport to its Kentish headquarters, a substantial penetration into the goods market was made, no great success in the passenger market could be achieved.

It was not of course for want of trying, but somehow or other the company never seemed in prewar days to find enough customers to offset the loss of what had been virtually a captive market, and even a concern such as Yelloway once having purchased four Leyland Tigers in 1931 could not be tempted to try the newer Maidstone products, despite the retention of the last of the Express models, until 1939 when they were commandeered for military service. This retention factor was also noticeable elsewhere, and perhaps one of its most amazing manifestations was within the fleet of the North Western Road Car Company to which we have already referred.

Its last Tilling intake took place in 1931 with the arrival of Nos516 to 545 inclusive, all of which were of the B10A2 type and had 31-seat bodies plus Nos546 to 577 which had a capacity of 35. From this time onwards Leylands and Dennis seemed to be the favourites, and one could be forgiven for coming to the conclusion that the Tillings would just fade away, but then, surprisingly, in 1935 over 130 were fitted with new Eastern Counties bodies. By the time the programme was completed in 1936, no less than 158 had undergone the process, a number which increased to 164 in 1939 when six bodies were transferred from their original chassis to Nos516 to 521 inclusive which were then in their 1931 state.

I was always surprised by the way in which these vehicles had been dealt with, for they were given high backed and most luxurious seats, curtains to the windows, heater units fitted behind the front bulkhead, controlled by a spindle which passed ther through and terminated in a substantial aluminium handwheel, parcel racks, a nice combination trim of plished wood, creamly imitation leather cloth and a maroon grey patterned fabric and doors to close off the almost inevitable rear entrance.

The rebuilding did not extend to the chassis, and so we still had that unmistakeable note from the engine, a none too sparkling performance, and often the retention of the single braking system but for all that, they gave us a most comfortable ride day after day, until eventually they were displaced by their Bristol successors. I particularly remember here how well they seemed to cope with winter conditions for in those days the only snowploughs one ever saw were drawn by a single horse, and if there had been a fall overnight of more than about two inches the effect that these equipages had on the highway surface was about nil. For all that, although I often saw the road littered with immobilised cars and lorries, a Tilling was not to be found amongst them unless deep drifting had occured.

What of course we did not know then was, that a third lot of body alterations would soon be upon us, and these came out during the war when perimeter seating became the order of the day. I loathed this arrangement, for 29 seats were laid out around the sides, or against the front bulkhead so as to give as large a floor space as possible and on to this could be crowded a considerable number of standing passengers. Perhaps it would be best if I were to refrain from mentioning the maximum number of persons that I ever witnessed on an Express under such circumstances, but I do recall wondering how the engine ever managed to cope with the load.

On reflection though, I ought to have been more concerned with the stopping power for the two rear brake assemblies must have been sorely taxed in view of the gradients which had to be negotiated on route, but the drivers never seemed to raise many, or any, objections and so they were kept at work until around 1945.

Let us now retrace our steps to 1937.

I did say a little earlier on that the company was unable to make any great success in the passenger market despite making some quite prodigious efforts and without any doubt the most important of these was placed on view during the period of the Commercial Show of that year. There were a great many public service vehicle chassis available for inspection at Earls Court, but without any doubt, the centre of attraction was the Tilling Stevens Successor. For, as a contemporary reviewer said, 'this represents the first British example of a practice which has previously been adopted in America and Germany although in the latter country it is now very commonly applied to railcars. This is the use of a flat diesel engine mounted under the chassis in order to gain the maximum floor area and seating capacity on a single decker'. From this, it may be correctly deduced that Tilling Stevens had built the first of the many single deck underfloor buses that are now playing such an important part in the psv world. Like so many of today's examples, this could accommodate 44 seated passengers but there were some important differences from what has now become accepted practice.

The power unit was an 8-cylinder horizontally opposed direct injection diesel engine which was designed and constructed within the company's works. It had a stroke of 98mm (very short) and a bore of 110mm with a total ouput of 95bhp at 1,650rpm. The crankcase and cylinder blocks formed a quite complicated casting with the necessity to incorporate wet type cylinder liners. Again, unusually, lubrication was on the dry sump principle, a separate 7-gallon oil

Above: Tilling rebuilt chassis number 6577 in pristine condition after being rebodied by Eastern Counties in 1935. This bus was broken up by its owner in 1939.

Right: The advanced Successor with Duple bodywork which was exhibited at Earls Court in 1937 as depicted in its bodybuilder's advertisement on the front cover of *Bus and Coach*.

Bus & Coach

The Operators' Journal

DECEMBER 1937 — ONE SHILLING

DUPLE

In Advance Again

In designing and producing the ultra modern coach illustrated, Duple again lead the Coachbuilding World. Tilling-Stevens Motors were responsible for developing the Successor chassis with 8 cylinder central diesel Engine and other outstanding features — Duple craftsmen were entrusted with the Coachwork of Britain's Most Modern Passenger Vehicle.

DUPLE FOR DISTINCTIVE DESIGNS

STOP PRESS.
During the official opening of the Earls Court Exhibition the following press comment was made— "One of the most striking things on show is the new Tilling-Stevens Luxury Motor Coach with a Diesel Engine" (*vide Evening News*).

DUPLE BODIES AND MOTORS LTD.
EDGWARE RD., THE HYDE, HENDON, N.W.9
Telephone: Colindale 6412 (Pvte. Ex.). Telegrams: "Duple, Hyde, Hendon." Cables: "Duple, Hendon, London." Codes: Bentley's, A.B.C. 5th Edition.

tank being fitted to the chassis frame. Another interesting feature was the provision of two fuel injection pumps which were horizontally mounted each feeding the cylinders on the relevant side of the engine. Behind the engine was a 16in dia single plate clutch and behind the clutch a 7-speed Maybach pre-selector gearbox. The operating level was mounted below the steering wheel and after the gear had been selected, it was only necessary to declutch when the assoicated ratio would be engaged by vacuum-operation dog clutches. Seventh speed was an overdrive which gave a maximum road speed of 47.5mph. The engine and gearbox were mounted as a unit immediately behind the front axle and carried by resilient supports.

From the back of the gearbox ran an open propeller shaft and here came then another unusual feature for two rear axles were provided, only the rearmost of which was driven in order to reduce any propeller shaft angularity. The final drive ratio was 5.8:1 and each rear wheel like its front counterparts had a brake drum and shoes, the latter being applied hydraulically with vacuum-servo assistance.

If I were ever asked to give advice to an 'up-and-coming' chassis designer I would present him with two maxims, these being — keep it simple — and what looks right is right.

Tilling Stevens had elected to give its new bus independent rear suspension using horizontally mounted coil springs for the purpose, whilst the arrangement adopted was relatively simple, it does seem to be somewhat peculiar and consequently one cannot help wondering just how it would have behaved in normal service, particularly as it never had the chance to display its characteristics.

There were a few other interesting features, for example a small propeller shaft came forwards from the crankshaft to the very front chassis cross-member where there was support bearing. Immediately behind the bearing were two pulleys, one at the front taking the fan drive belt (for the machine had a forward radiator) and this also passed round the pulley which drove the dynamo, this last unit being carried on swivel mountings so that belt tension could be properly adjusted. Here of course, was a throwback from the old Express Mk1 design. The second pulley on the centre shaft accommodated the exhauster driving belt and here again we had another unit that was both hinged and frame mounted.

Tilling Stevens built at least two of these chassis, one of which was bodied and a photograph of the complete assembly which included Duple-manufactured coach work appeared on the front cover of *Bus and Coach.*

It was also the intention to use the engine and gearbox in a goods chassis (it would have resembled the postwar Sentinels), which was to be known as the Yeoman, but I have been told that those power units which appeared at Olympia were incapable of running. Development work was continued and it is reputed that the process was an on going one until well after the end of World War II, but, as has been so often the case, operators seemed to be frightened by the unknown and there is no record of any one of these remarkable machines actually being sold to a commercial customer.

Certainly no reference was ever made to either the Successor or the Yeoman in any postwar publicity material but it is intriguing to surmise what might have happened had the link between Maidstone and the bus operating companies mentioned earlier not been broken in the early 1930s.

By 1939 the sight of a new Tilling Stevens bus chassis was becoming increasingly rare although they were still included with the catalogue and a few were bult for export of which odd examples came on to the home market during 1939 and 1940. Thereafter and for the next few years the company was involved in the production of searchlight generating sets of forms TS19 or TS20. This was certainly putting the unapproachable petrol-electric experience of the Maidstone staff to the very best advantage.

The generator sets used the four-cylinder 78hp petrol engine that had originally been manufactured by the Vulcan company, and it was in fact the Vulcan side of the business that re-emerged when civilian production restarted after 1945 so that by 1946 a six-ton chassis with either the same petrol engine or a Perkins diesel alternative could be purchased. Then a remarkable Tilling Stevens appeared which, perhaps in view of the prevailing fuel shortage, was a battery-powered five-ton goods model costing £1,595 and this in turn paved the way for a new series of TS passenger chassis known as the K range.

These chassis had a 17ft 3in wheelbase, remote-mounted five forward-speed constant mesh gearbox, an underslung worm rear axle, and triple servo vacuum brakes. The K6L had the Gardner 6LW engine, and was quoted at £2,066 in the 1950 Commercial Show guide, whilst the K6M employed the 10.35 litre Meadows unit and was offered at the slightly higher figure of £2,310.

Right: A Meadows-engined coach chassis in 1950. The power unit had a 10.35litre capacity.

Below right: A rare postwar bus-bodied Tilling-Stevens. A Meadows-engined Tilling-Stevens demonstrator with a Longford 35-seat body. Used first by Aberdare UDC as a demonstrator, it was later with Neath & Cardiff.

These machines, distinguished by their very deep radiators, could be obtained also with the Gardner 5LW and/or lefthand drive and in the main went for export, although some went to work as luxury coaches in this country when the K6M could be relied upon to give an outstanding road performance. Again though, none of the larger operators had sufficient interest to place an order and to the best of this writer's knowledge and belief only one was ever fitted from new with a bus type body designed specifically for stage carriage work, although there may have been other exceptions.

Prior to the 1950 Show however, yet another passenger chassis was introduced and this reverted to previous practice in being christened the Express Mark II. It also followed tradition in being rather underpowered as the engine was the Meadows type 4D 330cu in four-cylinder model which developed 80bhp at 2,200rpm, a surprisingly low figure for the time as the then maximum dimensions of 30ft by 8ft were employed.

A unit mounted five-speed constant-mesh gearbox of Tilling Stevens manufacture was fitted and this was perhaps the only lavishness contained within the specification as the whole vehicle, like its illustrious namesake, was seemingly constructed on the elimination principle everything being kept as simple and straightforward as possible. Even the triple servo braking system had been dropped in favour of the continuous flow hydraulic layout that was light and cheap.

As a result of all this the Express Mark II was able to compete in the cheaper end of the market for it sold at the remarkable price of only £1,395 but it failed to achieve the success of its predecessor and I well remember seeing the advertisement of a Leicester dealer in the trade press at the time that the concern was disposing of the last examples at an even cheaper figure following the cessation of Tilling Stevens/Vulcan vehicle manufacturing activity around 1951.

The company never really had enough capital in the later years to exploit its capacity and so it sold out to

the Rootes group at this time when approximately 25 chassis were being built each week and the order book was still being kept at a satisfactory level. By this time my old friends had vanished from the roads around Manchester for withdrawals began in earnest after the war once new rolling stock became available, a process that was completed by 1950, although by a coincidence in so far as these pages are concerned four were acquired by Holts of Rochdale a concern which owed its inception to the original Yelloway company. My last sight of one found it in a very unfamiliar situation... at the end of a tow rope and obviously being trundled through Deansgate Manchester en route for the breakers yard and now 25 years later the marque is almost forgotten.

If, though, there were no Tilling Stevens chassis there was a small consolation for the Victoria works still continued to produce automotive components and in particular the TS3 two-stroke diesel engine which was used in the Commer range of vehicles. This activity too had meant the appearance of the company's name at various postwar shows where the stand on the gallery used to display there units has been so labelled. It has therefore fared better than another company's former premises which in the late 1920s were the home of one of the largest commercial vehicle builders in the country. By yet another coincidence these same buildings almost became a branch of Victoria works as will be detailed in chapter IV.

I was sad to hear of the Tilling Stevens sale for it was through having to wait for a bus of that make that my eye was first taken by a tram, but here we are back again with that 'chicken and egg' situation, to be described further in the next chapter.

3 My Tramway Days

As I mentioned at the commencement of the last chapter the arrival of the new North Western Tilling Stevens buses made life a whole lot easier for the residents of our village for the nearest place with any reasonable shopping facilities was some three miles away, but my family like most others in the district went further a field when funds were sufficient, and at such times the inevitable mecca was Stockport.

The buses now made a choice of transport possible and so in winter we used the train, as stations then boasted such civilised conveniences as waiting room fires, but in summer took the bus, although I must digress a moment and mention those Saturday trains for they had some very bus-like characteristics. The usual arrival at the village station was a Sentinel railcar but from time to time the unique ex-Great Central petrol-electric machine would put in an appearance and this often gave the impression on the return trip that the gradient out of Tiviot Dale was just about as much as it could manage.

Something, though, must have gone wrong with the system on this particular night, for winter or no, we used the North Western service and so at around 7pm we were stood shivering in Mersey Square waiting for a sight of the Tilling Stevens that would tinkle us back home.

We stood on the steps of the bus building, which still stands just as it did over 40 years ago, only there were comparatively few buses about for the square was then honeycombed with tramway tracks and these were well occupied by both Stockport and Manchester rolling stock. The net result was that every vehicle in sight whether railbound or not was painted red and then all at once there came from around a corner a thing of beauty clothed in green. Before you could say Stalybridge, Hyde, Mossley and Dukinfield Joint Tramways and Electricity Board I was pestering my folks for a ride on this exotic stranger that diffused an air of moorland vistas into the somewhat restricted confines of the square, but a ride I did not obtain and so it passed out of my sight but not out of my thoughts.

I never have understood why I had not seen one before, or why I did not meet one on our later expeditions, but then my luck changed for Father took me one night to a bowling match and we started out by train changing on to a Tilling Stevens which was bound for Mossley (Brookbottom) at Greenfield station. This was new territory so I kept a sharp look out and thus espied what seemed to be tramway poles in the distance. Alas when we reached them (at what had been the Haddens terminus) I discovered that although the tracks they had once served were still in place the overhead had gone. Even so the track did not appear to have been long out of use, but then at our destination the line came to an abrupt end and for a few minutes I was puzzled as to the reason for its existence. I was also puzzled as to why 'Brookbottom' should be perched on top of a veritable mountain, and that I have still to solve, but I did solve the track problem when I saw an unobtrusive and partially tarred over trailing connections sliding out around a corner and away down a hill. Obviously any tram that arrived at this place had to reverse to continue.

I wanted to follow that track and later that night I did so, for we walked down the hill to Mossley station passing en route a branch to a disused depot, and there parked outside the booking office entrance on a length of bright and wired rail was my second 'Green Linnet'. I still did not achieve a ride despite some intensive pleading, having to be content with what the LMS — always a dubious outfit to my mind — later provided and so I returned home rather dejected but all at once thing changed for the better.

I was informed one Saturday that shopping was off — we were going out to tea — and there was a ritual that I detested, but then in the course of a discussion on travel plans one of my parents mentioned those magic words 'Mossley station' and life took on a much brighter aspect.

Well we arrived at that place around three of the clock and there once again stood a green tramcar with the driver draped nonchalantly over the front dash as he chatted to his mate who was leaning against that same piece of ironmongery, but alas the car was not for us, for they, horrible men, in response to Father's inquiry recommended a bus.

I watched the tram disappear and then a few minutes later our conveyance hovered into sight and what a sight. It was tall, short, and thin and bore the inscription 'Thornycroft' on the radiator and was in fact one of the Boadicea models produced by that firm. From the vintage look of the thing it had probably been ordered by that monarch herself. Neither the make ... My first . . . nor the colour did anything to assuage my disappointment and neither did a seat by the driver/conductor until I suddenly saw that the track which had carried my desired tram out of sight unobtrusively split and we began to follow an obscure branch which swung sharply to the left.

The second track was still wired and it went on and on but never a tram did I see, until Father suddenly saw his friend and we alighted. I recall that the afternoon for me at least was very dull until at last a trip to Stalybridge was suggested and then my eyes

Below: This may not have been the author's first Green Linnet but it was certainly the last. SHMD car No63, here posed at Hyde on 19 May 1945 after joint board tramway operation had been discountinued, was for years a frequent visitor to Stockport and Edgeley.

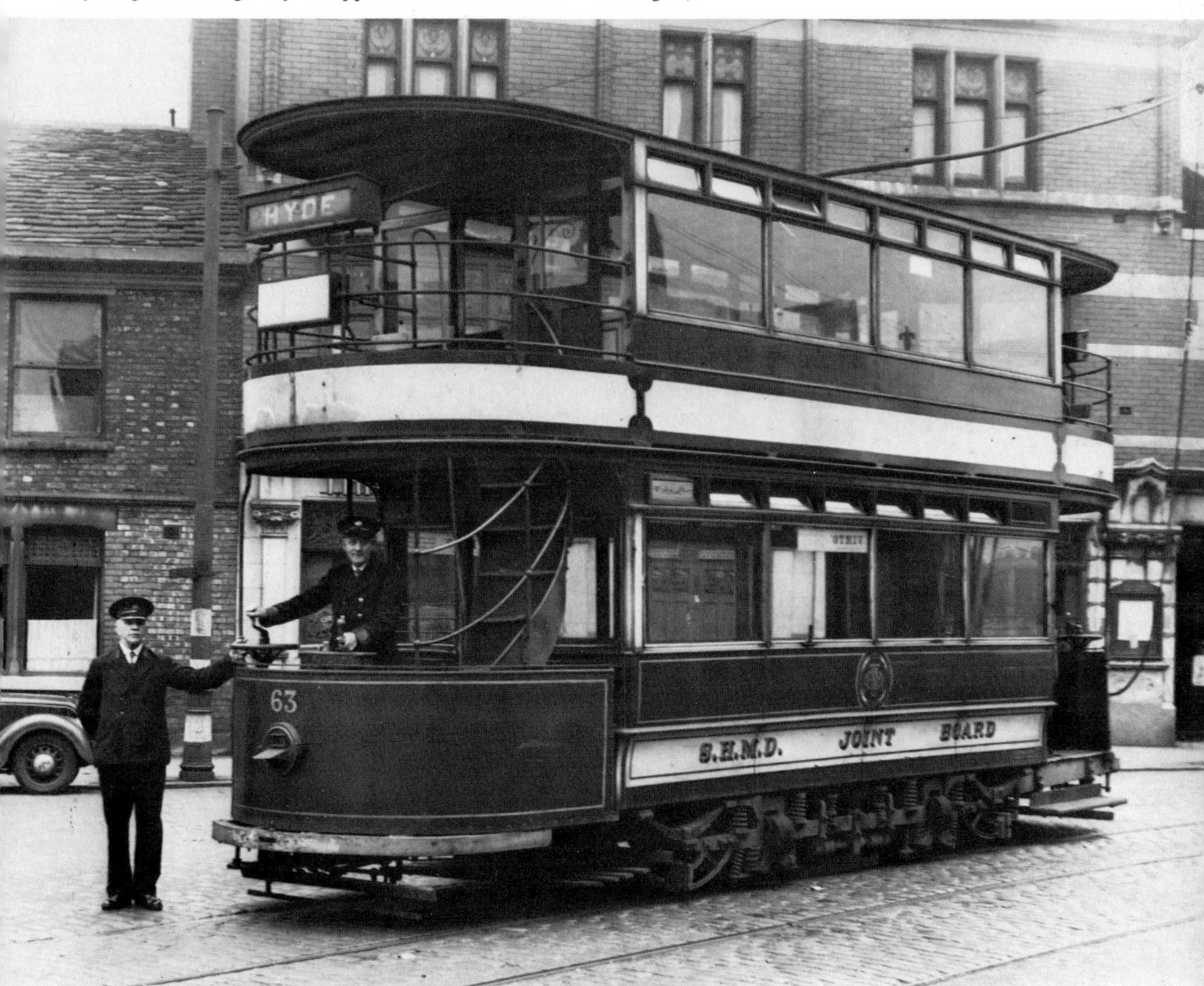

were first opened to the miracles of modern science.

Our hosts for that time were affluent for they possessed a radio receiver — and do I mean receiver. On the righthand side of the fireplace was a substantial wooden shelf and perched upon it was a large cabinet about three feet long and two feet high. From this sprouted two knobs and a cable, the latter leading into the base of the grandpappy of all speakers — a bronzy horn that would not have looked out of place on the end of a giant euphonium. After we had had tea the apparatus was switched on, the knobs delicately adjusted and out from the speaker came various oscillations, squeals, howls, plus ever so faintly in the background the measured and precise tones of the National news announcer, until suddenly the whole cacophony of sound was blotted out by a tremendous roar.

The lady of the house cried 'The tram, the tram.' I was thrown into my coat and out of the door, and there on the loop by the church of of St James

Left: Oldham market place circa 1930. The single track turn off to Henshaw Street and West Street just used by the No9 car in the background is clearly visible, as are the connections leading to George Street used only to turn cars, a ritual carried out fortnightly to even out tyre wear.

Below left: West Street was the terminus until June 1935 of the Middleton cars. Ex-Middleton electric traction No119 is well loaded even in this offpeak period.

Millbrook stood yet another Linnet. I can see its lights in my minds eye ever so clearly even now despite all the years in between.

The SHMD was like no other tramway system as it did not die. If just faded quietly away and the Haddens-Mossley-Millbrook-Stalybridge route was then in the fifth year of that process hence the absence of cars to Mossley Brookbottom. Now the all-day service on the Millbrook section had gone too, but trams still ran to Mossley Station each weekday morning and afternoon and also on Saturday evenings, although I believe that a more regular service was still running from Stalybridge as far as the bottom of Millbrook village, with some cars going into Ashton.

Well we boarded the car for what was undoubtedly the roughest ride I had had on a vehicle of that type to date. The noise and sway which only ceased to the slightest extent as we climbed Ditchcrot Hill were appalling and then we swung from side to side on the descent past Westhill School, until we reached the Mottram Road junction.

There we stopped to allow a car from Mottram precedence and so the two in convoy gained the centre of the town. I though Stalybridge was marvellous, particularly when we returned to Mossley via Black Rock and the route taken by my second and third sightings, but I had not then seen Dukinfield, for there was a place with a tramway on every street, and if some were then disused well it only added to the interest. Unfortunately by the time that I had penetrated to that portion of Cheshire the trams to Mossley were no more, the routes via Black Rock or Millbrook closing on 25 May 1935, and 29 June 1935, respectively, but the fading away process continued with the routes from Stalybridge to Hyde via the Alma Hotel and from Duckinfield to Hyde being downgraded from all day to part day usage, until the trams then 15 in number finally departed from Tame Valley depot in 1938 at a time when I was the owner of a bicycle and so able to gain some insight into how the various changes were being made.

Even this cutting off of the main trunk though, did not mean the end of the last branches for six green survivors (Nos 18, 42, 61, 62, 63 and 64) continued to ply between Hyde Market Place and Gee Cross until 21 May 1945 by which time only four remained in a serviceable condition and then this route, still gently declining, continued to be used by Stockport trams until they too were withdrawn on 2 March 1947.

There was, though, nothing gentle about the riding characteristics in the later days as the track had sunk to the level of that on the Millbrook route but there were other stretches I had known that were worse and so I must digress for a page or so and comment on my second favourites for nowhere have I ever seen any reference to them in print.

I first saw one shortly after the Green Linnet affair, when travelling on a Ripponden & District bus from Manchester into Yorkshire. These blue single-deckers were noted for speed and reliability but this day ours did not pass Hollinwood so fast as to make me miss the sight of a most antediluvian single-deck car parked outside the shed which then housed the Oldham Corporation car works. The building still stands virtually unchanged but now alas bereft of both track and tram, being a part of the Ferranti factory, for its transport service came to an end in 1938, following the opening of the corporation's large Walshaw Place bus depot.

The creature I had seen had numerous window pillars, open ends, and an immensely long trolley mounted on the roof clerestory. Like all Oldham trams of the time it was painted in the standard livery of red and cream, but these colours were somewhat unusual for it always looked as if to each pint of the original material was added a pint of brown so that the cream was brought to a biscuit shade and that of the red to a hue best described as oozy mud.

I had not seen anything like this creature before despite having passed through the town fairly often, but a little while later I saw another coming empty up the single track in Yorkshire Street with a prominent '3' on the route number blind plus the destination 'Mills Hill Bridge' and so further investigation was necessary. It was, though, little wonder that I had missed seeing the vehicles that performed on that route or beyond to Middleton as they terminated at the top of West Street and so were virtually invisible from the narrow and very congested Market Place that then existed.

Through this area passed trams on the main line which ran from Waterhead to Manchester or Hollinwood, together with the short working cars to the latter place which reversed in the High Street outside Woolworths, the routes involved being Nos20, 1 and 11 respectively. The High Street crossover was also used by the Hollinwood via Hollins cars on service 12 which quickly diverged to the left to travel via George Street, the points being worked by a boy who was housed in a form of sentrybox but he also had another set under his control for in the Manchester main line was a facing cross over, and this led straight on to a righthand turn out. These metals were used by the No9 trams from Shaw Wrens Nest to Chadderton Road, but no sooner had these gained the turnout and the foot of Henshaw Street than they had to cross the straight portion of yet another turnout which, if taken, led left to West Street and Middleton.

West Street was then very narrow indeed but it was just wide enough to accommodate a loop a little below the brow of the hill and here was the town terminal of the No3 service. The first car I saw there was a standard double-decker which, if painted green, thanks to its open platforms and Preston lineage, could, have been taken for a Green Linnet, but the next car in was a single-decker and this was identical to the one I had noticed at Hollinwood.

The main thing I noticed this day was the incredible load it carried, and on my subsequent visits I never failed to be amazed at the way passengers used any available space for their better accommodation, but I did not know then that only the single-deckers could negotiate Mills Hill Bridge, the double-deckers having to reverse at that point.

Neither did I know that my second favourites consisted of a batch of eight cars that had been built originally for the Oldham, Ashton and Hyde system in 1899, but when that concern was wound up in 1921 they were transferred to the adjacent and jointly-managed BET subsidiary known as the Middleton Electric Tramway Company. That process must almost have certainly involved the use of Oldham tracks but this is something I have never been able to ascertain properly for in those days the corporation only ran to the Free Trade Hotel at the Oldham/Chadderton boundary where there was a loop . . . and a gap.

At the other side of the gap was the terminal loop of the Middleton system and this was only filled when on 9 August 1925 Oldham took over its share of the Middleton system which consisted of the track to Mills Hill Bridge plus the aforementioned eight cars which became fleet Nos113 to 120 in their new owner's stock.

They must have been a dubious bargain but the track was a much worse one. Manchester Corporation relaid without delay everything contained in its part of the former Middleton empire but Oldham resorted to patching, although in some places there was little to patch apart from a series of haphazard grooves in the setted road.

Because of the bridge the single-deckers could not be scrapped but such were the affects of wear and tear that within a year or two some replacement stock was an absolute must and so, as a first essay, a standard double-decker No43 was turned into a totally enclosed four-wheeled saloon.

A second — No47 — followed, only this did not have windscreens, an omission that was rather surprising at first sight because three of the ex-Middleton trams, Nos114, 115 and 120 were so treated and thus gave me rather a shock when I first set eyes on one.

The track, though, gave me a greater shock and it was something of a mystery to know how the double-deckers kept to the road as they rolled and rocked through Chadderton, although derailments did towards the end become a regular feature if certain ex-tramway informants are to be believed. The last car ran on these services on 11 June 1935 when certain Crossleys to be mentioned in chapter IV took the road but by that date double-deck trams had begun to run through to Middleton as a new and higher bridge was rolled into place during the weekend of 14 December 1934. For years afterwards, though, a reminder of the old days existed either in the track or traces thereof which displayed the kinks necessary to keep within the limits of the original and very restricted arch.

Losing those single-deckers was saddening for single-deckers were so rare in that part of the world, but almost at the same time that they vanished I took a ride on utter modernity in the shape of a Blackpool railcoach and was highly impressed by their outline, performance, centre doors, and large boarding platform. Alas their length would have precluded their use on most of the SHMD system but there were other sections of tramway within the greater Manchester area that could have accommodated them. No-one, however, bothered to indulge even in an isolated experiment to prove their capabilities and so old age and the diesel engine overcame the resident population, by the end of the 1940s. By then of course trams were becoming rather rare, but a number did remain and some of these I came to know from the inside as it were, and this happy event followed a change of occupation.

My first operating employer had some trams but at first I saw little of them, being engaged in the task of revising the layout of sundry bus stop signs, until I was stopped and told to 'Get out a few drawings' for new construction was in the air. Well before you can do this a certain number of basic facts are needed. These can be summed up by the short but important questions of: How long? How many wheels? How many motors? How many decks? How many seats? How many doors? How much expense? and so on, but at this stage few answers were forthcoming.

Nevertheless I quite enjoyed drawing tramcars, particularly as I was being paid for the task, and so some very unlikely sketches were produced and laid before authority for inspection and possible approval.

These it seemed needed to be thoroughly digested and so by way of a starter it was decided to resuscitate a project that had died a year or two before and I was instructed to 'acquaint myself with the experimental car'.

I journeyed by tram of course — to the central works and here I had a nasty setback. I though I knew trams, but I couldn't find that one. The works office telephone operator, who was a mine of information on every local subject, said it was in the bodyshop and there I repaired but I still couldn't see any tram, and so I cautiously approached the foreman who according to rumour possessed a very hard centre under a very gentle pink and white countenance together with a reputedly bloodcurdling method of dealing with fools.

He listened to my request for information as to the missing vehicle patiently, and then sadly, or so it seemed, led me over to the most unlikely looking pile of scrap I had ever seen and said 'Its theer', when he could have fooled me.

The object of my search had set out in life elsewhere to prove that a tram circa 1931 could beat a contemporary bus, and so it did. The original owners then bought some new cars but not like that one which languished in an almost derelict state until my undertaking bought it for some obscure reason, as it had nothing that was even remotely similar amongst a very mixed flock. It did, though, gain a coat of grey paint on transfer which collected more and more grime until stage one commenced a few years before I became acquainted with it.

Now you should understand reader that a tram has substance, even if it has not a lot of style, and this one

Below: Night work. A Sheffield track gang engaged on heavy track repairs. The distance between the road surface and rail bed will be noted, but fortunately on this occasion at least a fine night has been selected.

Left: Light repairs? Little apart from the basic lower saloon structure remains in situ. But the dismantling process has left exposed the substantial platform fender and under bearers that render a tramcar virtually collision proof — unless it met one of its own kind.

Below left: 'Solidarity' is the only word which can be used to describe the under frame and framing being included in this new single-decker, note particularly the size of the corner pillars.

was built according to the book. It had an underframe made up of two 8in × 4in channels which ran nonstop from headstock to headstock and just so that it would never sag in old age each was secured by numerous countersunk headed bolts to a continuous chunk of ½in plate which was about 18in in depth.

These formed both a rocker panel and a base for the body frame of 4in × 4in timbers. There were numerous vertical pillars, and five horizontal members at ground, rocker, waist, ventilator and roof levels whilst the roof itself was made up of ½in tongued and grooved board covered with about seven alternate layers of canvas and paint. Then from the headstocks hung the platforms, but their bearers of 5in angle ran well back under the framing and so they could be tied additionally to a cross-member or two.

The whole lot weighed about 15tons and ran on two maximum traction trucks, only there was not now enough traction and so four motor equal wheeled bogies were substituted, but corner clearance trouble then ensued and so a little modification followed.

The whole body was stripped down to the skeleton and then two mightly men armed only with a hacksaw and a packet of blades went into action. They cut off each end, and the roof above, and then took out a two bay slice from the middle ending up with five pieces of tram. The odd numbered sections were then discarded, the even ones set up carefully on trestles and a dropped centre section let into the underframe, but just how delicate all this was can be judged from the fact that they did not attack the roof in the middle at all, and so its boards formed the only link between the two original bits.

At this stage the cutting party retired exhausted and never resumed, so as all the discarded chunks had been thrown inside the 'rump' perhaps I can be excused for not recognising what looked like a mouldering hen cote as a living tramcar, but live again it did, even if resurrection from the grave took all of three years.

Not all that time though was spent on this, our prime subject, we had other tasks too. The engineering side had always been divided into tram and bus sections and divided was the operative word. I often wondered why the respective works were not guarded by barbed wire, trenches and machine guns, for they were poles apart in evey respect, but eventually the bus faction became all dominant and rather had their eyes opened in consequence.

Take bearings for example. In a bus wheels run on rollers which are precision fitted. Big ends are even more precise, whilst the chassis components are provided with needle or ball assembles in profusion. Not so a tram. The truck bracketry usually blacksmith-fabricated might have the odd brass bush but then again it might not, and if it is so favoured then puzzle: 'Find the grease nipples?' As for the all important axlebox bearings, well it is perhaps best not to inquire into fitting methods for a bit of slop is useful on a curving track, but in any event the machine used for bearing boring was not just as accurate as it might have been.

There were, of course, other bearings on the axle which carried the traction motor, together with a large gear wheel which meshed with the motor pinion. These gears were encased in a sheet metal housing and this was usually filled with a thick sludgy compound that went under the colloquial description of 't'fat'. The gear teeth had doubtlessly been machined in the days of yore, but those were long past, and despite the action of the aforementioned lubricant certain wear had taken place which gave rise to those sounds which denoted the approach of a tramcar from afar.

Not unnaturally therefore the bus brigade being brought up in an atmosphere of dedication to tighter limits began to set a few for the tramcars and sundry drawings began to appear that were dimensioned to three places of decimals, but I do not think it can be truthfully said that any worthwhile improvement occurred on the older rolling stock which continued to grind and clatter along the track and there was another experience.

Few enthusiasts spare much thought for track but they should. A length of even light tramway rail is difficult to handle whilst a section such as 8C is downright intractable. It has to be laid to gauge, bent in flowing or transitional radii and this is bad enough in one plane. Let a curve coincide with a change in gradient and a second bend is necessary in a second plane.

This applies to normal rail, junctions are another matter althogether.

When a big junction was to be renewed a survey was taken and a precise plan produced. This was then sent as part of an inquiry to one of the trackwork producers who would send in a price and eventually a tender would be accepted.

Then a representative of the chosen firm would carry out a second survey and from that came the drawings for each separate piece. As junctions were largely made from manganese steel each single point

and crossing had to be cast from individual patterns so the time and expense involved can well be imagined and once a piece had been cast alteration was well nigh impossible.

At last, though, all the bits would be delivered marked up to a key plan, and a permanent way squad would have a jolly time in the yard making sure it all would fit together, it was a sort of jig-saw in excelsis. But if it did fit a weekend would be chosen and on the Thursday night half the road surface would be dug up and replaced by some very temporary filling. The second half would follow on the Friday and all was then ready for Saturday and some hours of very intensive activity which would begin around 10pm when out would come the filling. As this was taking place the new rails would be coming up from the yard on bogies in the proper order and stacked accordingly and then as soon as the last service car had passed the much augmented district gang would dash in and cut and remove the old junction wasting no time on that part of the procedure.

Once it was lifted the supporting concrete bed would be swept clean, examined and any patching neccessary carried out using quick drying cement. Then the new rails could be swung into place, a mobile crane having been purchased and very useful it was too, when each was fishplated and laid on big wooden wedges. The fishplate bolts though were left loose so that by knocking the wedges in or out the rail could be brought to the required level and then an 8in bank of gravel would be run along either side so as to form a trough. Into this would be run some molten pitch which both held the rail and provided a resilient bed. The tie rods were now adjusted for gauge, the fishbolts

Above: 'Ready for re-assembly'. It tooks from the condition of the tyres, gearwheel and bracketry that car No122 is about to receive a new truck. Lifting demands a good headroom and no conflicting overhead.

Right: 'Danger men at work'. Swinegate depot Leeds was a hive of activity when this picture was taken. Passengers seldom spare a thought for the vast area of glass which has to be cleaned nightly on both sides of every psv.

would be tightened and the road surface, or as much of it as possible, put back, and it was really at about four in the morning that one would discover just how well that survey had been taken and just how well the parts had been made to the dimensions so deduced. As I have remarked tram rail is a difficult medium with which to work and one could not afford to have a gap of two or three inches at the end of a work that could cover anything up to 150ft or so.

The vital factor was, of course, could the first scheduled car pass on the Sunday morning, but not only dimensions came to be involved here as I found out one night. Trackwork, thank heaven, was not my forte but I never objected to seeing how other people tackled their problems and so I became involved in a survey or two and they were an exciting business as motorists never had much time for tramway tracks and seemingly even less for those engaged in perpetuating these antiquated monstrosities.

Anyway from these forays came the invitation or command to participate as an unskilled assistant in one of the Saturday night revels that were still being held — and quite frequently so — at this time. It was quite a big junction and we began as nine struck on the Town Hall clock one balmy summer night, that season obviously being the most suitable, although its choice was invariably dependent not upon planned desire but such other factors as committee minutes, council decisions, the size of the department's purse, the manufacturer's delivery promises and, perhaps most important of all, the realisation thereof.

By 10.30pm the road was well and truly dug up, but a cloud or two had formed in the sky and by the time we had begun the task of sweeping out the foundations there was no doubt as to what was going to happen. It did too. There came one flash, one bang, and a torrential summer storm followed.

We had an excavated area of around 70ft long and 16ft wide which, sad to say, lay at the foot of a valley. Down the slopes on either side came the three double connecting tracks, and down the tracks came no less than 12 separate and quite considerable rivers of water until we had a 12in deep paddling pool. We had aquatic sports that night all right. The wooden wedges floated, you couldn't see where the gravel was and the pitch solidified almost as soon as it came to be immersed, and I became immersed too as one happy soul handed me a pneumatic impact wrench and gave me the job of lighting up a few dozen submerged fishplate bolts for experience.

It was an experience to remember and the wonder was that nobody ever seemed to catch a cold through working all night in sodden clothing and nobody — except one — seemed to have any thought of returning to a sport. The other wonder was the number of people abroad in that City Centre despite the weather and I can add for the record that there was not a single tramway enthusiast among them.

Sad to say the activities of the night gang did not always meet with the approval of the neighbours, particularly so if compressors or pneumatic drills were in use. One of my friends was tucked up in bed one night when his phone rang, and so grumbling and bemused with sleep he staggered down to the hall to answer it, wondering who on earth could be calling at two in the morning. The voice at the other end did not

Above: 'Postwar construction'. New bogie cars for Aberdeen nearing completion in the Wishaw shops of their Pickering builder.

reveal its identity but it did growl 'How do you like having your sleep disturbed as ours has been all week...?'

My friend, even more bewildered, tried to ascertain the cause of both the call and the question but the person then rang off. He needless to say returned back to bed only to be aroused again by another voice about 20 minutes later.

It was about two hours and 10 calls down that he found the reason. A group of neighbours in a certain suburb had been disturbed by a relay and decided to get their own back on the person they thought was responsible namely the tramways manager. Alas for my friend he lived in the same district and had the same name only he did not hold that office, but if he did not appreciate the mistake that had been made it is to be hoped that the incumbent did when he heard the story.

I had one or two other runs and then for a change a romp or two with the lofty individuals whose work was on a high plane, namely the overhead wire men. This came about because an old service car was to be converted into a repair vehicle when the centre of the saloon was cut out to accommodate a tower and operating winch, and I was landed with the design of the necessary equipment. I came away very surprised at what was involved, there was far more precision and danger than I had ever imagined and here again was a job that invariably had to be undertaken in the dark and in inclement weather. It was, in fact, a relief to return to a nice warm office and break any monotony thereby involved with a trip down to the bodyshop where we had another conversion in hand.

Another batch of secondhand cars had been purchased, and these proved to be heavy both on the track and themselves. The track suffered through their axle loadings, body sway, braking equipment, and sundry other defects, whilst their weight played havoc with bolster and axlebox springs, so it was decided to effect a little lightening by a spot of decapitation when a double-decker would be singled.

A pretty sketch of the result was drawn up in all innocence and work began — but not for long.

Up to this time I had thought that my anticipated

piece-de-resistance was a well-built tramcar but now I knew it was actually of the flimsiest construction. These other monsters had metal-framed bodies and the frames of substantial angle iron were riveted together with fastenings having been provided on a most generous scale. The only method of dealing with them was to centre punch and drill each one, then cut off the head with a big hammer and set chisel and finally knock out what was left. It was soon realised that this just was not on, and so the section that had been stripped had the panels replaced and the car crept back into service in its original guise, just as if the attempt had never been made.

It was on one of this batch that I did my first-ever conducting turn. There was a 'do' on in the park which coincided with a staff shortage and so some press-ganged innocents volunteered to lend a hand and here some discrimination was practised — the girls were allocated to buses the boys to trams.

We had about 10sec training in filling up waybills and using a ticket machine, were handed a fares chart and then told to acquaint ourselves with it in our standby time.

In my case the standing was not of long duration and in no time at all I found we were to be engaged in some short workings from a traffic interchange point to the main gates, a distance of around one mile. We shuttled to and fro taking about 100 passengers a time up the hill for a couple of hours and then we brought them all down again. The income in terms of pence per that single mile of route must have been enormous.

My mate and I then had a break but being keen types agreed to go out for the rest of the night on long distance, a trip of about three miles each way from the City Centre to the Park.

Now the afternoon car did possess straight stairs but after tea we received an old timer with a 180deg turn type of ladder, and it was then that I found just how much physical work was involved in running up and down them. By the time we made our last depot run I was worn out and I seem to recall spending most of Sunday in a hot bath trying to eliminate a certain stiffness in the joints.

Now and again when I become involved in certain productivity discussions I cannot help thinking that presentday conductors don't know what work is. It's a far cry from seven passengers a mile — roughly today's average — an Ultimate (or some other sophisticated machine) and a nice bus staircase, to the 15-passengers per mile of a tram, two racks of bell punch tickets, and those incredibly hard iron-shod stairs, on of course running times that were not all that much different plus the task of trolley turning at the terminals, or having to remember to hold the rope at turnouts and even doing a sprint behind the beast after putting over the points at some of the more remote junctions, when care had to be taken not to distribute your takings all over the highway.

At least though the exercise kept you warm — being on the front end was very different. I was taught how to drive during a period of night work to be mentioned later. My tutor was one of the foremen and he first took me out on a genuine old timer with an open front that was then being used on service duties.

We had the main roads to ourselves and so there was not much chance of my hitting anything, even if the handbrake was well past its best, but my how, cold it was, whilst I found driving in the rain to be particularly trying. I then wondered how regular drivers such as those on the SHMD had fared in winter when working long turns on the more exposed routes but apparently they preferred the open life.

In actual fact that undertaking did once experiment with a vestibule at one end of just one tram but its life was incredibly short, and so perhaps it was no coincidence that the employees of my concern never liked to do a turn on the few remaining open balcony cars as they always maintained that even with the traps in place the draught that swept down the stairs was enough to cut a body into two.

Reverting to the subject of the experiment, there should not have been any such problems on this car which by now was looking less like a pile of scrap for it had separate cabs. We actually started on the frontal appearance and here we had two problems. Firstly the vehicle was just over 41ft long, and this meant that the ends had to taper so as to provide clearance on various tight corners. Secondly as this car was strictly a 'one off' curved glasses could not be entertained so we had to work in flat sheets, which proved to be somewhat difficult for it was necessary to place the pillars so that there would be room in the cabs for any size of driver.

Here, though, the foreman who became a much respected friend proved to be a tower of strength and he made sure that the tram displayed the same characteristics by looking over my first layout and suggesting that we used the same timbering dimensions as had the original builders. 'Make it strong boy and put in the windows tight' was his advice and he was right, particularly in so far as the glass was concerned.

When we reached cantrail height we met another snag . . . that of matching up to the tongued and grooved roof, and so we schemed up an aluminium dome that provided quite a modern look, and incidentally the waist rail and window lines were arranged to follow tradition by conforming to the appearance of the more modern trams within the fleet.

We had quite a time with the body as management wanted a combination internally of polished wood with a contrasting Formica and, as the use of the latter material was then in its infancy, we were rather involved in some development work.

Many of the body fittings had to be adapted either out of what there was in stock or designed so that they could be made up in the workshops as simply as possible and a case in point here was the light fittings which were let into parcel racks. These were fabricated in the tin shop and then sent out for stove enamelling, and we were similarly involved with the seating, when turn over transverse units purchased second hand from another source had to be altered to meet the new seat rail and floor trap dimensions.

By far the most involved work though went into the running gear. Because of the weight, the underframe had been arranged as I have mentioned to run on two two motored bogies, but in the interval of time which had elapsed since work had been suspended and restarted these had been employed elsewhere. The car thus came to acquire a pair (which had 27in wheels) purchased from another undertaking and now there was insufficient clearance so two 2in substantial packing pieces were made up to lift the whole vehicle accordingly. The new bogies had solid bolsters with a brass rubbing casting carried on a rubber buffer at their outer extremities. These castings had to bear upwards on to sector plates which had to be wide and long enough to allow for the travel and throw out involved when negotiating the sharpest curves on the system. Mounting these sector plates necessitated the adaptation of the main cross members which also had to be set apart to allow for access to the bogie king pins, and additionally they required drilling for the cables to pass through to the motors. These cables incidentally ended in substantial wooden boxes mounted under the longitudinal seats flanking the centre entrance and we also used the seats to accommodate the sand boxes.

Sanding at first was another problem until I had an idea and went to see an acquaintance of mine who was involved elsewhere in the maintenance of another form of railed transport and returned with an ex-Great Central Railway steam sanding ejector. We made a mock up and found to our delight that this would deliver sand to the rail when given not steam at 180psi but compressed air at 90psi, and so another trip was necessary to purloin three more. There truly was a 'Gortonian arrangement' and perhaps this was the only tram ever to include parts intended for a Jersey Lily for I am sure the Grimsby and Immingham cars were never so equipped.

Brakes were the next problem. We started off with a pair of brake valves which originated from where I cannot remember but these did have a sanding trigger mounted over the horizontally-operating application lever. We also had air wheel and air track brakes on the trucks together with a secondhand compressor and a serviceable governor, but additionally emergency brake valves were needed on either side of the entrances. It was necessary to see exactly what connections every single piece needed and then work out a piping layout as installation progressed. We also followed motor bus practice by putting the compressor on to six resilient mountings, and that was a worthwhile improvement, even if the output pipe then gave some difficulty until a crafty crank or two provided some flexibility.

The trucks had originally been under a conventional car and had interconnected hand brakes. Turning the handbrake spindle at either end wound up a chain (shades of Marley's ghost) which was attached to a substantial shaft.

This was pinned centrally to a waybeam to which was also attached a pivotting equal lever the whole being rather similar in appearance to the conjugate valve gear of a certain H. N. Gresley but from either end of the equal lever ran two adjustable rods to each of the bogie brake beams. The whole lot was designed so that both sets of brakes could be applied from either end and till work whether the car was on straight, curved or downright kinky track and here we passed. It was going to be very difficult to put this lot in a dropped centre and in any event we needed the space for the air supply reservoirs, so the trucks were in effect reversed so as to bring the waybeam to the outer side of each rather than the inner, and a single connection was then run to the hand brake spindle via the inevitable chain. The handbrake assembly possessed another in-built snag as due to the restricted amount of room in the cabs a small radius handle had to be employed and we overcame the lack of leverage/braking power by putting some gearing into the foot of the pedestal together with the usual pawl and ratchet. To the best of my knowledge and belief no one ever had any handbrake service problems with that car.

The cabs had to accommodate quite an amount of equipment but fortunately the controllers were of modest dimensions being designed for use on the electro-pneumatic system. They like all the rest of the traction system were secondhand but the electro-pneumatic contactors were mounted in a substantial frame which had been intended for mounting under a curving staircase with plenty of headroom and we had nothing similar, so the frame had to be reduced to the maximum extent possible and then squeezed into the only room available, but this meant providing some reasonably weather proof access traps which could be lifted off without too much time being spent in the process.

The contactors were supplied from a low voltage system which was fed from a tapping off the air brake compressor motor and this was backed up by a

Above: '10 years too late'. The first British VAMBAC-equipped car was No208 in the Blackpool fleet. Note the resilient rubber wheels and large track brake shoes. Current consumption was high but the original US PCC specification demanded automboile standards of acceleration.

Right: VAMBAC roof-mounted controller as fitted to No208. The coil springs return to swinging actuator arm back to the off position being connected to this component via the single roller chain.

battery which joined the sanding gear under the longitudinal seats. The battery was a new one and so were the two resistances but they had to be. Again as space was at a premium we only had one area left and that was on the roof so up they went.

Also on the roof was the current-collecting gear and here again we ran into space difficulties as it was impossible to employ long tensioning springs. No solution was in sight until someone suggested we visit a spring manufacturer who was located remotely 'up country' and yet reputed to possess a great deal of practical talent. So it turned out, for in about two days our inquiry was turned into a set of springs which possessed tapped adjusting bobbins secured into each end by the coils and thus was another solution achieved.

It was fascinating to see how that unlikely pile of junk was turned into a reasonably attractive vehicle despite the relative slowness of the process for almost all the work was done by just two body makers, two fitters, one electrician and one electrician's mate, this being all the labour that could be spared from the main task of keeping the rest of the operational fleet operational.

Almost equally fascinating was the study I was able to make of the contents of the department's archives for contained therein was a large collection of drawings which had been amassed over a considerable number of years, and in it were general arrangements of such gems as Manchester Pilchers, Darwen streamliners, Liverpool bogies, various London specimens and even the Cardiff lowheight four-wheelers but one very important concern was quite omitted and that of course was the SHMD.

Nevertheless just looking them over made one realise that the day of the tram had almost passed but it was a fairly close run thing for our pet secondhand Rosie became the foundation stone of a development programme that nearly achieved production status. Through this we were shown just how it would be possible to eliminate all the clanks and rattles one associated with tramcar operation by having shaft drives, resilient wheels, hornless trucks, rubber bushed mountings, proper lubrication systems and all electric braking, and there can be no doubt that some very impressive engineering was involved.

Had it come 20 years earlier tramways might still be with us en masse but it was all too late as I was forcibly reminded during a certain interview that I shall never forget. I was asked the question as to what sort of work I was then engaged upon and mentioned a few of the things detailed in the preceeding paragraphs when my questioner snorting and incredulous exclaimed. 'Trams! Trams! We scrapped those "B" things years ago. Tell us what you know about buses'.

I took the hint and the next opportunity.

As a result I never took part in the actual process of launching, but some years later I had to change trains and having an hour to spare took a walk along some very familiar pavements. I had not gone far when I saw a rather special shape approaching and so I ran to the nearest stop and booked to the terminal. The performance and ride ón tracks that were then about to be finally scrapped were far better than I ever expected, and I came away feeling sorry that such a lot of work should really have gone to waste, but we seem often to go round in circles so perhaps this might yet not prove to be the case and I shall have the chance to put the experience I gained to good use on a rapid transit system.

If we should though be on a circular course I hope that I shall never be faced with the sort of problems that some of my predeccessors had to overcome at the time when I saw my first Green Linnet, for their perseverance and ingenuity must have been quite incredible.

Below: The last new tram to enter service in this country. Leeds car No601 at Torre Road during its first trial trip on 11 May 1953. This machine had conventional electric equipment.

4

Produce of Huddersfield

From time to time we used to leave our Derbyshire home and journey on to the edge of the Pennines to visit certain relatives and this usually meant travelling on three different buses. The first would be the inevitable Tilling which would take us in to Manchester and once there we would make for the basin of the Rochdale canal hard by what was then London Road station, but now renamed Piccadilly.

At that unlikely spot would be found bus number two, the blue Leyland of the Ripponden & District Motors concern, working on the hourly service to Halifax and Bradford which would take us to the edge of Oldham and there would be bus number three or perhaps three and a half if size was anything to go by.

It was usually a three-axled double-decker and usually of Karrier manufacture, being not one of those pale shadows lately made by the Rootes group but a true native of Yorkshire, built in Huddersfield when the company was one of the big names in the motor industry.

It had not, of course, always been like that for the firm which was founded by the Clayton family in 1907 was in a very small way of business prior to the commencement of World War I.

In 1913 however it had produced a design which met the War Office subsidy scheme requirements and once hostilities began large-scale production was put in hand, with the result that by the time the armistice had been signed four years later over 2,000 of this four-ton model had been produced.

As we shall see some military activity continued into peacetime, but the commercial market was now the all-important centre of attraction and consequently the limited range of charabanc and bus chassis that had been offered prior to 1914 was considerably augmented. Perhaps, though, overwhelmed might be a more accurate description and certainly any storekeeper who had to deal with Karrier parts stocking over the next decade could be so described.

It would seem that things started off very quietly and the first model to sell in any quantity was the very conventional CL4 which boasted a normal control layout, high radiator, crash gearbox, and a very long bonnet, but as the latter was largely full not of motive power but empty space there was always a noticeable lack of urge apparent.

The engine was of the four cylinder side valve pattern with a capacity of 5.2 litres (4½in bore x 5in stroke) and this was made by the firm in Huddersfield, but even if it was not fast it does seem to have had the desirable merit of reasonable reliability.

Other features of this beauty were the inevitable cone clutch, an underslung worm drive rear axle, single rear tyres, and no front wheel brakes, but to make up for this omission a transmission brake was provided which was coupled to the foot pedal and included, perhaps in deference to best tramcar practice, a pair of cast iron shoes, which applied the stopping effort to a steel drum.

The rear brakes were slightly more civilised for they, worked by the usual hand lever, had asbestos-based linings, but in those days engineers did not have to contemplate the merits and demerits of woven or moulded materials for there was just no choice. When a shoe wanted relining you popped into the stores, and sawed the necessary length off a coil of belting which was already and waiting for the purpose. Rumour has it though that this was not a process that took up a good deal of time for linings only wear out as a result of being worked, and like a certain Crossley this assembly had a spot of geometric trouble in the linkage, so as a load went on, the handbrake went off, which was all very confusing to the driver.

That worthy as a rule was the sole crew member on this type of vehicle which had a seating capacity of around 26 and, as such aids to convenience as Ultimate machines were unknown, he dispensed bell punch tickets and change as he dodged around the country lanes or between the local tramcars, keeping all the while an eye open for the odd tricks of their pilots, for in those days there was almost a state of war between the tram men and their bus colleagues. More than one local Karrier had the misfortune to be trimmed down from about 7ft 6in wide to around the 7ft mark as a result of being caught in a spot where the rail and kerb virtually coincided. All purely by accident of course.

Despite these troubles, and a nasty tendency for the chassis to droop where the bonnet met the body, these Karriers had fairly long lives by the standards of the time and as the 1925 price for a complete bus was in the region of £1,060 they probably represented an economical purchase which is more than can be said for the next endeavour.

This had its origins in the memories of the mud of Flanders, for about the same time that the CL4 was put into production the Karrier three-axled gun tractor appeared and obviously made a sensation, although whether or not the impact was sufficient for the military chiefs to dash off a few orders is something I have not been able to discover, but why the three axles?

If you look, reader, at photographs of the early CL4 machines you will see that they like many other contemporary buses have only single rear tyres. Now pneumatic tyres in the 1920s were by no means as immune from punctures as those produced today, nor could they carry the same loads, so there was every

incentive to add another pair if at all possible but this does not entirely explain the three axles, for twins could have been employed.

The prime reason was that with singles tractive adhesion was very much reduced, a significant factor in an era when most road surfaces consisted of smooth stone sets, often well laced with highly polished tramrail into the bargain, but more important even than the ability to start is the ability to stop, and no one had really solved in a satisfactory manner the problem of fitting front wheel brakes. Twin rear axles naturally provided a home for a second pair of drums, to augment the microscopic power previously offered, tram type equipment not withstanding.

Thus the multi-drive principle was one around which the motor manufacturers of the period made great play, and as Karrier was then vying with Guy for the honour of producing the first passenger rigid six and already had the gun tractor in existence it is not surprising that it became the foundation stone of a new line of buses.

Left: Some of the earliest Karrier products were charabancs. This H type demonstrator only dates from 1924 but it would be a star attraction could it but appear at a presentday rally.

Below left: The local Huddersfield concern naturally took a large number of Karriers right up to the end of the company's existence. CX 5355 was another early post World War I product, being based on the CL4 chassis which was reasonably reliable despite a small engine.

Below: CL4 motive power; a good deal of space remained under the bonnet cover when the four cylinder side-valve engine had been installed. The klaxon horn, autovac and the high level dynamo drive are typical of the period.

The first prototype was suitably promoted sales wise after completion, and is shown in an accompaning illustration along with Wee Georgie Wood, a wellknown music hall artist of the day, who perhaps had been recruited to show potential customers just how easy it was to start.

The first gus (yes gus not bus) ran around until the experimental department was satisfied and then passed as registration number CX8989 (chassis NoCY6-5052) into the hands of an operator not a hundred miles from Huddersfield for a spell of service in the field and there earned for itself the apt nickname of 'The Red Lettuce'.

Why? Well it was painted a bright red, and when it was running it would not, according to the locals, pull the skin off a rice pudding. The power such as it was came from a Karrier engine that was similar to those in the CL4, but by the time production of what now became the CL6 had got under way this was dropped in favour of the 5.9 litre Dorman model 6JU, and that would have given Georgie quite a sweat had he ventured a second try.

Starting was a real problem, so much so that in more than one garage men would spend every night in winter or all day Sunday going round the bays and running up their occupants so that they never had the chance to go cold. If they missed one then the methods applied varied with local knowledge and equipment, from towing, through the four-man trick... one delicately manipulating the carburettor controls, two on a rope fixed to the starting handle, and one brandishing a flaming torch around the air intake... to the ultimate in self-starters. A fiendish device this, always home made, and comprising one surplus tramcar motor fixed on an armour plated bogie complete with controller, and trolley. You put the latter on the nearest tram wire, hitched up the motor dog to the starting handle, stood back and switched on, when anything could happen.

When at last there was some response the troubles had only just begun, for they consumed oil and petrol at a fantastic rate, so not only were the sumps checked by the engine oiler each night but that worthy also put a two-gallon tin in the cab for good measure — and use in the afternoon... if it ran that long! Still if it should continue all day then anything from two to nine gallons of lubricant could be required.

They also had another endearing feature in that big ends could be knocked out in the bat of an eyelid, and this, mark you, in the days when crankshaft bearings were of white metal running on soft steel, and fitted with a great deal of scraping on a highly individual basis; but if a big end did not fail then you could bet the gasket would.

As most bus garages were improvised in tram sheds fitters spent a good deal of their time below ground in the full length pits, either freezing in the icy blast that blew down from end to end, or well warmed up if they dropped one of their tram voltage pit lamps into the water that usually lay up to 6in deep, but not all their efforts were confined to the front end.

It was not then appreciated that twin driving axles needed three differentials, but these buses had only two so the wind up stresses set up between the axles led to half shafts snapping like carrots. For a time these were replaced as they broke until it was realised that is was far simpler... and cheaper... to take out the offender's partner, blank off the axle ends, and continue on a single drive.

Being thoroughly modern buses resulted in the inclusion of air brakes (but not on the front axle) and these can be described as interesting for a truly progressive brake valve was then still an ideal for the future. They were thus either all on or all off, and the sudden effect of a crash stop, or indeed any stop made by any but the most delicate-footed and experienced driver was quite something. One of my friends who then worked for Karrier stoutly maintains to this day that one of the first test runs ended in the demolition of a Huddersfield cottage that had the misfortune to be in the way of the supposedly deaccelerating CL6, but be that as it may.

There never was any doubt, though, that the compressor drive, a small diameter shaft connecting that component to the timing chain via some even smaller rubber couplings was very much on the tishy side, and as replacement had to be undertaken through a small trap in the front bulkhead it was also the cause of a good deal of bad language.

Carrying on rearwards we next meet the rear bogie brake linkage, of imposing form but fitted with almost inaccessible grease nipples, unless the body was removed which is not a normal service operation, and at the power end of the linkage were the diaphragms, also of rubber, and also subject to rapid failure. When one blew the lot had to be changed otherwise brake balancing was quite impossible.

These two factors plus the brake valve had their effect upon the suspension, for leaf springs have to accommodate both the starting and stopping torques, but here we meet another snag. The rear springs had a central pivoting frame mounted fastening, and were secured to the axles at either end. Consequently when one broke — there was no if here — the bus would drop down till the wheel arch came to rest on the tyres, and then someone had to bring the lame duck home. This was achieved by crawling underneath, inserting a jack and packing under the frame, lifting, and then inserting a piece of wood cut for the purpose between the axle top and the bottom frame flange.

It will be realised from all this that the fame of the CL6 soon spread and perhaps as a result only about 30 seem to have been built in the model's two-year production run, but perhaps this lack of popularity could also be ascribed to the fact that a buyer parted with around £1,300 and then only ended up with a 26/28-seat bus.

Something bigger was obviously called for and it soon arrived as the WL6. The WL6 was big in everything including appetite and its Dorman engine could gobble up petrol at the rate of about four miles to the gallon. This characteristic led to some peculiar refuelling methods, and in more than one town the mid-morning would see men armed with a stack of petrol tins awaiting at the various central termini for the buses to come in when the tanks could be replenished. This performance seemed to last until the patience of local constabulary was exhausted, and then mobile petrol tankers became the order of the day.

This enlarged engine was the Dorman 6.59 litre 6JUL (80bhp at 2,000rpm) with a bore of 4in and a stroke of 5½in and a repositioned compressor, only its former space was now taken up by the water pump which was again shaft-driven, and again prone to shaft failure, so that, in my boyhood memory at least, the WL6 which performed on our local route was invariably shrouded in steam.

One of my relations who drove them was a big man physically, but even he had difficulty in handling the gear lever which was just as far from the non-adjustable driver's seat as it could have been and believe it or not he could not reach the bulb of the horn, so every time he wanted to sound that piece of equipment he had to rise from his perch and reach over the top of the steering wheel! Perhaps this was just a local hazard, and in the event he much preferred these normal control specimens to the others.

The others, of course, had forward control, so that the driver received the full benefit from a well heated cab side plate plus copious petrol fumes, but these came in two further varieties double or single-deck and

Above right: Huddersfield's later forward control Karriers were of larger size. No37 (chassis NoKL562) was one of six machines (fleet numbers 33 to 38) to enter service in 1926. It was later sold to a travelling showman and was last licensed by him in 1938, presumably being scrapped thereafter.

Right: 'The six-wheel era'. The first six-wheel CL6 single-deck demonstrator outside the Karrier factory main gate. The passengers are not what one might think from a first glance.

HUDDERSFIELD
HUDDERSFIELD CORPORATION TRAMWAYS.
No 37
CX 8157

1917
"KARRIER" SAFETY COACH.
057 CX

Above: Liverpool, too, became an enthusiastic Karrier user. Its first six-wheeler was purchased in 1927 and by June 1928 42 single-deckers and 6 double-deckers were in use. This example comprised a WL6 chassis at £1,119 plus £53 for an electric starter, and had a Liverpool-built body. Note the tram-like appearance of the latter and the way in which the autovac has been built in the front bulkhead panelling.

the former he hated with an intensity that was almost terrifying to behold.

The corporation had a nice selection of double-deckers and all had a fully floating cab, or at least the front sides and floor did the floating as the canopy type roof came out of the body. This meant that a gap had to be left between the two parts, and this gap in theory was sealed with a pice of rubber, but it was not long before it either perished or became torn away, so whenever he had one on a wet day, and these are not unknown around Manchester, his first task was to hang up his greatcoat on the windward side so as to keep as dry as possible.

Like most of his confreres he was a handy man, and as he always firmly intended to return to depot each night he carried an assortment of spanners with him. I suppose too that he included in his arsenal the inevitable length of curtain spring. The reason for this was that the buses had autovacs with quite small top tanks. When running up hill at full bore, the petrol usage rate was greater than that at which it could be sucked up, but some Pennine slopes are several miles

Above: 'Mystery Bus'. VH 2446 (chassis No42141) seems to have had a peculiar history. First registered on 16 July 1929 as a bus, it was recorded as being in use in the Newcastle area as a lorry only six months later, but was never again relicensed; although the tax was paid by Karrier Motors it could have been an experimental vehicle and so scrapped early.

long. This meant that if the driver was not very careful in the way he used the accelerator the supply would peter out, and then out too had to come the spring. A piece of rag was tied to it and dipped into the petrol tank, when the top could be taken off the autovac, and the sodden material squeezed out to provide sufficient liquid to give a full float chamber and hence a start.

Here he had to be a big man, for the doubles had been delivered with electric self-starters, but no one in that era of depression could afford such luxury and so they were all *removed* as an economy measure. Apparently certain well-defined principles were involved here in that when a driver reported for duty in the morning he received a going Karrier, and it was his responsibility to keep it in that condition, so if he should stop the engine and there was no convenient down grade to let gravity have its head, recourse to the handle was the only choice.

The double-deck contingent could be subdivided yet again into two distinct varieties, the earlier WL6/2 type, and the later DD6s. The former were enlarged varsions of the enlarged WL6, and like them possessed the Dorman engine with all its idiosyncrasies, but the DD6 had a very different form of unit in the shape of a Karrier product which was distinguished by having sleeve valves. This meant that the tell-tale plume of blue exhaust smoke was invariably discernible from the exhaust pipe, but as the Karrier company had not resorted to the double sleeve it was never just as dense as that which left certain local Daimlers, nor ever quite as pungent.

This engine, which when first shown at the Commercial Show was without pistons also, had a few unpleasant tricks up its sleeves. One was the tendency to shed fan blades at very low mileages and a flying fan blade can be quite a destructive instrument. Another was for the timing chain to jump over the sprocket teeth when the timing and crank went out of phase, with peculiar results.

Then behind the engine was an even larger cone clutch, and this not only when working took itself up with a rush but from time to time did not work at all. It would jam in engagement, and the method then was to remove the cover plate, borrow the nearest available plank, and bump it out. You could do this as the

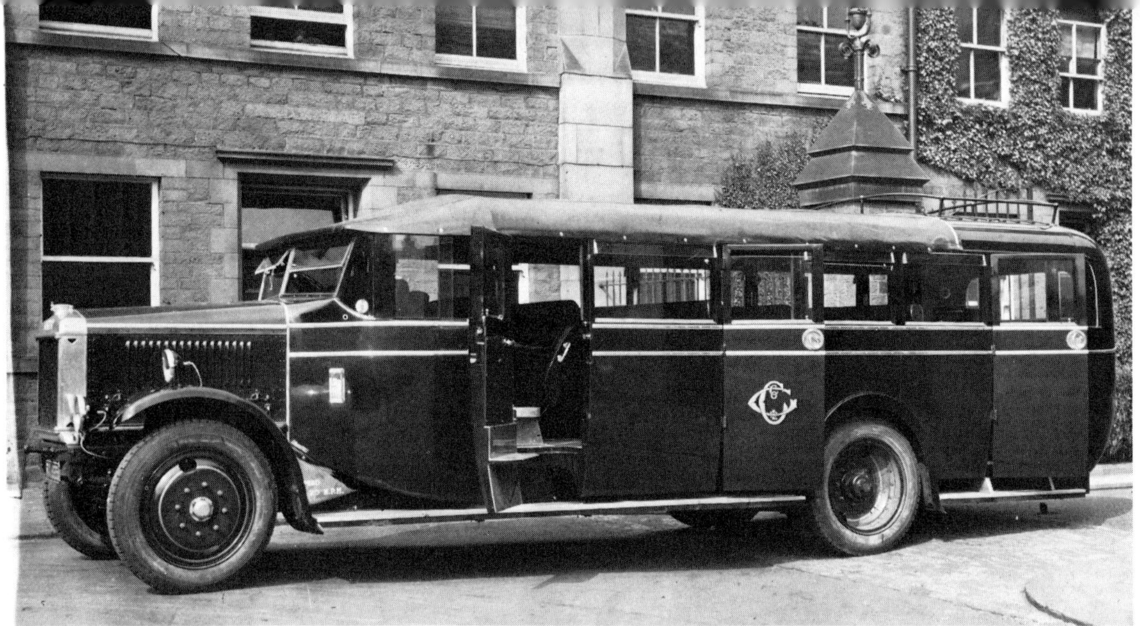

gearbox was remotely mounted, and coupled to the clutch mechanism by a short propeller shaft, but this advantageous feature came to result in a most appalling disadvantage as will be illustrated later in this tale.

The gearbox was still a very much crash affair, but from my inquiries does not seem to have given a lot of trouble, and rather surprisingly neither did the steering, despite the fact that these buses had a most imposing appearance and perhaps the largest seating capacity of any psv ever built until the arrival of the Atlantean over 30 years later. Because of their size the air braking system had wisely been retained but the control valve had been subjected to some modification, and was now a little more sensitive except in the initial stages, for after the pedal had been pressed there was a delay period before things began to happen of about three seconds, and that in certain circumstances can seem to be a lifetime.

I remember them well because as a child two features made a big impression upon me. The first which I loathed was the high front waist rail across the driver's bulkhead, so that although from the front seat I could look out sideways I never could see ahead, which usually spoilt the pleasure of a journey as adults would not always go upstairs. The other impression was one of sound, and came from the rear axles intermediate propeller shaft which suffered from galloping spline wear, and rattled along merrily in consequence.

Left: The influence of the charabanc remained strong until about 1930. This 'all weather saloon' features a canvas hood, roof luggage rack, three nearside doors, running boards and virtually no driver visibility over the enormous bonnet.

Below left: Huddersfield No105 was another machine with an interesting history. Its Park Royal 56-seat body was mounted on chassis No47023, the whole being licensed on 3 June 1930 although it did not enter passenger service until 2 August. Relatively few of these buses were built and their lives were not long. No105 passed into the hands of a London dealer and was broken up by the end of 1933.

Differentials still gave trouble, so much so that one fleet engineer, who is now retired but happily still very much in circulation, told me only recently that he had a daily parts delivery service arranged with the factory in the latter part of 1928 when his charges numbered just six, but what they lacked in quantity was more than offset in other directions.

My informant, to whom I am most obliged, turned up a most fascinating book in which he had kept a daily job record, and the extract for one machine read as follows:

14 May 1928	Bus delivered brand new.
16 May 1928	Bus placed in service
16 May 1928	Engine seized.

It was then out of commission for several days.

26 May 1928	New clutch fitted.
2 June 1928	Clutch slipping.
3 June 1928	Fan belts burned, dynamo shaft seized up.
7 June 1928	Fan belts burned, new belts fitted.
11 June 1928	Foot brake defective.
15 June 1928	Gear lever broken off.
26 June 1928	Foot brake defective.
8 July 1928	Engine seized up.

It was then out of commission for a lengthy period.

9 August 1928	Gear lever broken off.
12 August 1928	Hand and foot brakes defective.
16 August 1928	Broken spring bracket.
19 August 1928	Propeller shaft couplings failed.
25 August 1928	Exhuast pipe renewed.
27 August 1928	Air brake faulty.
28 August 1928	Jumping out of gear.
29 August 1928	Air brake diaphragm failed.

and then on the 2 September the engine shed its fan blades.

The Karrier employee who had the job of making the 200-mile daily delivery excursion was engaged in this task for about 12 months and then he obtained some very quick promotion becoming the general manager of a municipal transport system ending his career 30 years later still in the same capacity but with a larger undertaking in his care. After his retirement I came to know him quite well and once chivvied him as to why he had never bought a Karrier chassis. His reply was short and very precise, but then he had seen it all from the inside.

Most of the defects contained on the above list were regarded as typical but one unfortunately could only be described as potentionally lethal. That was the propeller shaft coupling failure, which was caused by a piece of peculiar design.

Both single and double-deck vehicles had the same sort of transmission layout, the flexible coupling flanges being secured by three studs on 120deg centres, but whereas those in the former machines were turned from $\frac{7}{8}$in bar the latter came from $\frac{5}{8}$in stock although generally speaking larger engines were involved.

On 8 August 1931 the almost inevitable happened and a most tragic accident resulted. A man and his wife were travelling at the front of a six-wheeler and on nearing their stop rose from the lower saloon seat they were occupying and made for the rear platform. As they were passing along the gangway two studs in the back joint of the short shaft which linked the engine with the remotely mounted gearbox sheared off but for some strange reason the third held.

The shaft was so short that it came below the dimension which made the fitting of a safety bridle mandatory and thus there was nothing to stop its flail like action. The gangway floor was ripped out, just when the lady who was behind her husband was crossing that particular space and as can be imagined the results were distressing in the extreme.

The whole of that fleet's Karrier double-deck content was taken out of service there and then whilst the remaining Karrier machines — a pair of two-axled JKLs — followed very shortly afterwards. This unhappy incident did not help and it came at a time when Karrier fortunes were somewhat in the melting pot.

The year 1929 had seen a full range of passenger chassis being offered comprising the then new Coaster, Cutter, Consort, and Chaser models. The Consort was the double-deck machine, whilst the Chaser was intended for 32-seat single-deck bodies and had only two axles.

The latter was reputed to be a speedy machine even when a four-cylinder engine was fitted, but it certainly had an odd quirk or two if the stories told by one of the foreman at a depot in which I worked were

Oldham Corporation was a confirmed three-axle chassis user having both Guy and Karrier products. WL6 No35 was new in April 1928 and had a 70-seat body. Note the engine oil cooler fitted at the foot of the radiator.

2
MARKET PLACE
KARRIER
BU-5172
35

Above: 'The last full size Karrier?' VH 4256 was a Chaser 6, had attractive bodywork and was new on 7 June 1932. It is not recorded as having been scrapped (by a Carlisle operator) until 13 June 1950 and so most surely have been the last of its line, although its later years were spent apparently on non-psv duties.

Below right: Diesel Power. Huddersfield buses Nos153 and 154, chassis Nos33047 and 33048, were of the Chaser 6 type but had Gardner 6LW oil engines with Northern Counties 32-seat bodies. They entered service on 11 November 1932 and lasted until March 1939 when they were sold to a Leeds dealer. Miles run in the 6½-year period amounted to 149,000 and 123,000 respectively. They were registered as VH 4759 and VH 4760.

anything to go by. He had a store of Karrier lore but the single Chaser 4 purchased by the undertaking concerned was his *bête noire.*

One of three saloons of different makes purchased for comparative trials, it and its fellows were put to work on a heavily-trafficked route that ran on a road across the valley from the premises at which he was then stationed as a running shift mechanic. As a result it was in sight of base for about a quarter of the total journey and in hearing for almost the whole trip, and this was just as well.

He and his confreres would follow its outward progress and if it had not been sighted returning in a reasonable space of time would then jump into the Ford T van kept for their use and go to the suburban end of the route where, unlike the town end, reversal was necessary.

The bus had a four-speed constant-mesh box and the drivers not unnaturally would select reverse after unloading, waltz round into the side street stop and then try to come forward again only to find that no other gear could be selected.

The shift mechanics, though, had the answer. A jack under any rear wheel and once the tyre was clear of the road surface apply a rocking motion forwards and backwards whilst the driver who would have been previously instructed in suitable terms did the same to the spring-loaded gear lever. Three times on average was all that was necessary before a 'click' announced that the gear train was freed was once more but it was all terribly time consuming.

This only happened when a new man was in charge, for the older hands had found the trick of pushing down the clutch and going from reverse to first whilst the vehicles was still rolling and if you did that no outside assistance would ever be required.

The same gentleman was sent one day in 1930 to Huddersfield for some parts for that same vehicle which was then just 12 months old, but he returned to report that the model was now regarded as obsolete and so no stock was being kept. It is therefore not surprising that its end came in 1934, a year which saw the end of the Clayton interest, but in the intervening space of four years much had happened.

On 3 August 1932, the announcement was made of an intended Karrier/Tilling Stevens merger. The new concern T. S. Karrier Motors Ltd was to transfer all ex-Karrier patterns, tools, jigs, patents, and manufacturing processes to Maidstone retaining only a small spares and service depot in Huddersfield and that was only to continue on a very short lease. A capital of £240,000 was envisaged together with a board of eight directors half of which were to be drawn from each of the two companies.

Shareholders of the Karrier concern ratified the deal at meetings held on 26 August, but five days later it was dead having been killed by their own board, although both the managing and sales directors were to have been drawn from the ranks of that body. I do not know why this decision was taken but wonder if the company had decided to pin its faith on certain new models, and the oil engine, for the 1932 range included various improved chassis (and they certainly were) noteworthy among which were the Chaser 6, the Monitor with a 110bhp petrol engine intended for 48/56-seat double-deck bodies and the three-axled Consort now re-engineered and boasting a Gardner 6L2 engine.

The Gardner was also put into goods vehicles, and then in 1933 came some two-axled passenger chassis of straightforward design similarly powered. Huddersfield Corporation purchased some single-deckers and was so satisfied with the result as to standardise on Gardner engines until the outbreak of the 1939 war; but, despite the foregoing, the considerable success of the articulated three-wheel Karrier Cob mechanical horse so beloved by the main line railway companies, and an ever increasing market for the reliable Karrier trolleybus, previous policy decision and the effects of the slump resulted in the purchase of the goodwill by the Rootes Group in 1934.

The Huddersfield works then was closed, when the Karrier name was applied only to trolleybuses built at the former Sunbeam company's Wolverhampton premises also a member of the group and to the range of lightweight or municipal machines based on the Commer range and assembled in that same Midlands factory.

From 1934 Karrier internal-combustion engined passenger vehicles started to disappear with startling rapidity, and by 1939 they were virtually non-existent. A postwar survivor was even rarer, but according to the Huddersfield motor taxation authorities the shapely single-decker shown here was not reported as being withdrawn until 1950 and so must have been one of the last if not the very last British survivor.

I seemed originally that only one solitary example remains, and its existence was revealed in a letter to the Editor of *Buses* which was printed in the issue for Novermber 1970. The writer who lived in Campbelltown, New South Wales said he had found a disused Karrier WL6/2 in a shed 'up country' in 1966. This was the only one of the type to go to Australia and it was shipped out in 1928, to continue in service until 1940 when it was withdrawn as a result of the then-prevailing tyre and fuel shortages. Its long period of retirement obviously caused some deterioration but now it is being restored to working condition. Surprisingly, though, a second Karrier was found in this country and it too is to be brought back to working order.

One tangible memento still exists in this country, though, for on the wall of a former factory building fronting on to St Thomas's Street, Huddersfield, is a large carved facsimile of the Karrier radiator badge that lasted as long as the marque. Memories also remain of an era that has now gone for ever.

If ever you have the opportunity to do so, ask one of the older generation of fleet engineers to tell you of his experiences, and you can bet that if he ever had anything to do with Karriers you will be in for a recital of events that might seem incredible. If you should doubt what you are being told reflect on the statement made by a colleague of mine, now retired, who was so involved. He read over the first draft of this chapter and handed it back to me with the comment 'Very interesting and very true. In fact if you had deliberately set out to design a bad bus you would never have thought to have included some of the troubles that we experienced.'

I must, though, in all fairness end by saying that the development work done by firms such as Karrier was really of inestimable value for there was a world of difference between the bus of 1925 and 1935 and so whether the industry realised it or not around 1930 better times were certainly coming, and with them the diesel engine.

5

A Comet Called Crossley

One bright morning I was surveying the world from my garden gate vantage point when the sight of an approaching double-decker made me stand up and stare for this was something quite out of the ordinary. It could at a glance have been mistaken for a North Western bus thanks to the red and white colour scheme employed but unlike that company's rolling stock in pre-Leyland Titan days it had a covered top.

It approached like a comet, which burst on the world, reached great heights and then faded away and that is just what transpired, for this automotive star was a comet, a comet called Crossley and it came into my view when the firm's fortunes were definitely in the ascendant. Prophetically again as it reached our frontage it broke down, and so I had ample opportunity to survey this wonder through the rest of the morning. It must have been one of the first if not the first Crossley double-decker to be built being either a red demonstrator or a member of the similarly-liveried fleet obtained by Manchester Corporation for the historic No53 route tramway conversion and so had a lowheight body and a petrol engine; but just who was the builder?

Crossley Motors had been formed as an offshoot of the stationary gas and oil engine manufacturers Crossley Brothers in 1910 around four years after the parent had started to build motorcars, and these soon earned a solid reputation for reliability and good finish.

During World War I the company became a major supplier of military vehicles to the Royal Flying Corps (later the RAF) and one extensively-built model was a utility/tender based on the 25/30hp car of peacetime and powered by a 4¼ litre side valve engine. Many of these after 1918 passed into civilian hands to be rebuilt as 14-seat buses, a typical example being portrayed in the first illustration and it is interesting to recall here that the firm of Plaxtons of Scarborough placed a very high proportion of its output upon Crossley limousine chassis in the early twenties.

Crossley cars flourished at that time, the Prince of Wales using them on his Australian tour, but the directors must have felt that there was little scope for profit in the luxury market, and no hope thanks to lack of capital to pursue Ford production methods and so break into the cheaper field. They therefore sought another outlet and apparently found what they were looking for in the summer of 1928 when the Crossley Eagle chassis was announced.

This was the Gorton firm's first fullsize psv product and as a result it was widely discussed in the trade press of the time.

The chassis frame was of the pressed steel type swept over the front and rear axles to provide a low loading line. The engine, a four cylindered 5.2 litre unit (bore 4 5/16in by 5½in stroke), developed 47.5bhp at 1,000rpm and was set to the nearside in a subframe to give room for the driver in the forward control type cab. The drive passed through a single plate clutch to the gearbox and that was carried in yet another sub frame which meant that the clutch was open and that a very short gearbox connecting shaft had to be exployed. The box was of the crash type and the gear change lever was contained in a gate which was mounted on the offside of the driver's seat, a position that was shared with the handbrake lever.

Braking equipment was provided on all four wheels, and had vacuum assistance, the main servo motor being located on the offside chassis member, between two of the twelve chassis outrigger brackets that were provided as standard to assist body mounting. At the rear end of the 16ft 7in wheelbase was a substantial rear axle unit with an offset differential pot containing an underslung worm drive gear, and the axle possessed the distinct advantage of being built to the fully floating pattern so that in the event of a half shaft breaking the attendant rear wheels were not likely to leave the vehicle. Fully floating axles were by no means universal in passenger chassis of 1928 vintage, and this up-to-date outlook was also followed in the transmission line for the propeller shafts were in two open sections and supported in the middle by a large centre main bearing.

Orders were soon forthcoming, Leeds City Tramways being an early customer taking four, Manchester Corporation purchased six, and a long distance Norwich concern, Norvic Coaches, put one to work on its London service and must have found the spare wheel, which was neatly accommodated at the rear within the chassis members which were splayed out to give the necessary space, very useful as a consequence.

Total output spread over a two-year production period was slightly in excess of 70, a figure which was not bad for a newcomer but before it ended it was obvious that wider horizons were contemplated for in May, 1929 the pioneer Crossley double-decker took the road and this really was a pointer to the future.

The vehicle was based on the standard Eagle chassis that still retained the 5.2 litre engine, but the springing and chassis frames were stiffened up to take the additional weight most of which resulted from the rather angular Roe-built 51-seat body, and one can only assume here that although the Gorton company was by now engaged in single-deck psv coachwork construction it did not feel sufficiently experienced to manufacture the rather special design that the Leeds concern produced, for this had the overall height of only 13ft 6in.

This dimension was achieved by putting all the upper saloon seats, 27 in number, back to back and having both nearside and offside gangways, a feature that was clearly reflected in the appearance of the lower deck for the ceiling swept downwards through concave and convex radii from the centre to the sides to provide sufficient headroom in the gangway but not over much above the heads of the 24 passengers there accommodated.

The significance of all this did of course lie in the fact that Manchester's new general manager Mr R. Stuart Pilcher proposed early in 1929 the tramway scrapping programme that is linked to his name. This programme began with the elimination of the famous No53 route where a whole series of low bridges prevented the use of double-deck cars. A bus at 13ft 6in could, however, pass under these structures so clearance was going to be no problem at all, but the service carried a fantastically heavy traffic, so, although the route had no gradients of any note, one big question obviously remained. Could the 5.2 litre engine cope?

The answer must have been in the negative for

Below: This blue and white vehicle posed against a typical Pennine background is based on an ex-RAF Crossley tender of World War I fame.

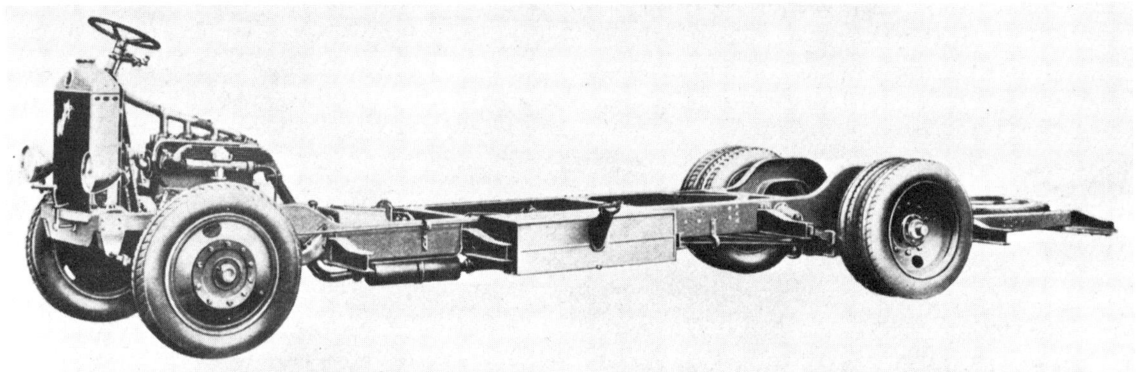

before long a revised range of chassis came out commencing with the single-deck Alpha and completed in 1930 by the almost identically engineered double-deck Condor, both of which featured a new six-cylinder power unit. Manchester then took 55 of the former and 20 of the latter (hence my sighting) double-deckers, finally effecting replacement of the tramcars in the April of 1939. Only the latter, whilst retaining two upper saloon gangways, were provided with transverse seating, instead of the back to back units that featured on the prototype.

The Condor cost £980 in 16ft 7in wheelbase form. The engine had side valves, a 4in bore, 5½in stroke, was rated according to the RAC formula at 38bhp (6.8 litre) and in actual fact could put out 110bhp at maximum revs. Other equipment included a vertical carburettor, high tension magneto, single-plate clutch, crash gearbox still (frame mounted) with a righthand gate change, and a 35 gallon tank, this being of particular importance as a Condor on city service would gobble up petrol at the rate of 4 miles to the gallon when on form, whilst usage when the engine was cold and the starting air shutter closed must have been too fantastic for words.

This factor though had not escaped Gorton notice and the next step in view of the Crossley Brothers association with heavy oil and gas engines followed predictable lines, for in May 1931 Crossley Motors publicly announced, what was then common knowledge in the trade, that its bigger bus chassis could be fitted with oil engines of Gorton manufacture.

In actual fact the first Crossley to be so powered was a conversion undertaken by Leeds City Transport which put a Gardner 6L2 into a Condor of 1930 vintage and for a time the chassis builder toyed with the idea of doing likewise on a production basis, but in

Left: The first full-size Crossley of 1928. A side view of the four-cylinder petrol-engined Eagle chassis.

Below left: The first double-decker. The modified Crossley Eagle fitted with Roe lowbridge bodywork having upper deck back-to-back seating.

the end came to the conclusion that it could not really support what in some respects was a competitor (over 100,000 Crossley Brothers engines had been sold by 1931) and so put its own design in hand.

The result was a power unit that looked as if it had been designed by a 'cubist', in fact, to paraphrase a wellknown advert, it looked queer, sounded queer, and by golly it ran queerly, although its advent was accompanied by strong references to all the testing that had been undertaken both on the bench and on the road. This was actually design number II. Mark I was a converted petrol engine which soon, despite increasing the crank diameter from 2¾in to 4in, demonstrated that it was too light bearing wise to withstand compression ignition pressures of around 800psi.

Mark II testing work had been carried out with the aid of Manchester bus registered VU 3668 which was noteworthy in being fitted with a 20 gallon gravity feed fuel tank that must have completely obscured the forward view from the lower saloon nearside front bulkhead window, but as that quantity of fuel now gave 280 miles running or 14 miles to the gallon at only 4d per measure whereas petrol then cost 1s, such unfortunate inconveniences had to be tolerated.

The engine was of the direct injection pattern with a bore of 4½in a stroke of 6in and a capacity of 8.35 litres. It had two separate heads each covering three cylinders with wet liners, steel asbestos gaskets, an electric coil (of 70 amps rating) in the induction passage to help starting and a compression release device intended also to assist the same process. In fact the contemporary publicity mentioned the presence of a CAV electric starter but went on to add rather optimistically that 'hand starting is a feasible alternative', a very dubious statement that would not have been possible had the Trade Descriptions Act then been law.

Other features of note were dry sump lubrication, a seven bearing crankshaft, overhead valves, and a Bosch fuel pump with a separate govenor unit. Output varied from 58bhp at 1,000rpm to 86.8bhp at double that speed and when one compares this to the capacity there was obviously going to be scope for improvement, although maximum revolutions came very close to producing smoke and unburnt fuel throw out.

Manchester Corporation was sufficiently satisfied with the conversion to order five new but basically similar oil engined Condors, whilst Stockton and Rochdale elected to take one each, and these orders were quickly completed as deliveries were then made in around eight weeks, which compares incredibly with what I have said about the same situation today in Chapter I.

The interest taken in the oil engine at the time was immense, the technical press was full of favourable comment, and as Crossley was the first manufacturer to offer a complete diesel decker ie engine, chassis and body, many inquiries were received, although putting in an oiler added £250 to the purchase price.

At the 1931 annual general meeting of the company the chairman, Sir Kenneth Crossley said that orders for psv work to the value of £250,000 were in hand and certainly by the middle of 1932 the list of firm customers was surprisingly large. There were 12 municipalities involved alone, most wanting oilers.

Manchester had by then indented for a total of 66, Barrow was taking a 6 and a 9, Rochdale called for 42, Ashton had a repeat order in, whilst Liverpool and Portsmouth began with single trial machines. The export market too was involved as a single-decker was about to be shipped to Perth, Australia, whilst two conversions carried out in Hong Kong had been so satisfactory as to ensure the placing of a repeat order for three more.

Many of the buses mentioned above were to have Crossley bodies and perhaps the most unusual of these were the five 48-seaters built for Bury which had doors at both the front and rear, and hence twin staircases. These made history as they all went to work on one route, which thus became the first ever to be completely covered by that type of engine.

Alas the comet was at the top of its orbit, for sales after 1933 began to flag and perhaps the reason was due to Crossleys being too quick off the mark and so not doing sufficient development work. Leyland started later as did AEC whilst Gardner had had years in the field and it is noticeable if one studies the various orders that once an undertaking had purchased any of these engines they seldom went back to Gorton — not before 1946 that is.

By 1933 Manchester was the only substantial customer but in that year three things happened. Firstly the manufacture of petrol-engined Crossley buses virtually came to an end, secondly a new oil engine came into use which had indirect injection but retained a capacity of 8.365 litres, although the bore was altered from 108mm to 113mm and the stroke from 152.4mm to 139.7mm. Thirdly almost immediately after this engine came a modified chassis named, not surprisingly in view of where it was sold, the Mancunian, that city soon acquiring a sizeable fleet.

PASSENGERS INSIDE OUTSIDE
CARDIFF CITY TRAMWAYS & MOTORS.
WILLIAM FORBES. General Manager

Above left: Early production model. The original print of this Crossley built for Cardiff Corporation and fitted with a more normal lowbridge body was date stamped 11 March 1930.

Left: 'Crossleys en masse'. This picture taken in the Rochdale garage in the early 1930s shows part of the extensive Gorton-built fleet once owned by that municipality.

Above: 'The Mancunian'. The first of the six buses of the type acquired by Oldham Corporation for tramway replacement purposes and powered by the VR6 oil engine. Bodywork in each case was by Chas H. Roe Ltd.

Some however did go to other customers and amongst these was the municipality of Oldham on whose outskirts we were living when the first of its intake took the road in the May of 1934, as fleet No57. This undertaking was then about to begin a four-year tram scrapping programme and this commenced in earnest 13 months later when the routes between Middleton and Oldham Market Place and Shaw Wrens Nest and Chadderton Road were abandoned — events that occurred on 11 June 1935. I was in the town the following day, and have never forgotten just how many buses there seemed to be in evidence, something that was hardly surprising as 42 vehicles had been obtained to cover these conversions, plus that of the Hollinwood via Hollins route that occurred on 21 December of the same year.

Thirty-seven were Leylands, but Crossley had obtained an order for five repeats and these like number 57 had Roe bodies, although the capacity was reduced from 57 to 52 the pioneer being altered similarly later. Full details are as follows:

Fleet No	*Reg No*	*Chassis No*	*Engine No*	*In Service*	*Withdrawn*
57	BU 7495	91746	?	9/5/34	?
1	BU 8421	91794	91797	6/6/35	27/10/50
2	BU 8422	71795	91802	7/6/35	12/10/50
3	BU 8423	91796	91799	6/6/35	12/9/50
4	BU 8424	91797	91798	7/6/35	9/2/51
5	BU 8425	91798	91800	7/6/35	9/2/51

The Crossleys in general and 57 in particular became favourites perhaps because they looked odd, but as their bodywork was identical to that fitted to most of the Leylands (some had English Electric coachwork) this state of affairs obviously stemmed from the chassis appearance which certainly had an old-fashioned air.

They had large diameter steering wheels carried on well-raked columns and ponderous radiators which, together with the bonnet sides that were inevitably hanging loose, seemed about to leave their mountings as they rattled over the cobbled streets. I did not know then much about technicalities but something still sounded to be odd if the engine note was anything to go by, and I should mention here in passing that although vacuum brakes were fitted there was no exhauster on the power unit. The necessary negative pressure was produced by engine suction and a throttle valve was provided in the induction piping. They had an air of their own and this atmosphere of distinction was retained when the Crossley Streamline model was introduced into the Manchester fleet commencing with bus number 601 of 1936 vintage.

The Streamline, which took its name from the modernistic contours of the associated Crossley bodywork had what was really a new design of chassis whose distinguishing feature was a new radiator that combined the traditional Crossley Mancunian shaping with a much neater chromium-plated seal.

According to contemporary literature the Streamline was the subject of a continuous process of development and so let me describe the sort of machine that was coming out of the Gorton shops immediately prior to the commencement of the 1939/45 war.

The engine was now known as the 47/99 diesel and was entirely of Crossley manufacture, the basic dimensions were a 127mm stroke with a 113mm bore which gave 6 cylinders a capacity of 8,365cc. Power output was 99bhp at 1,700rpm and it was alleged that with suitable gearing one could obtain a road speed of 45mph which could have produced quite a few excitements. The design incorporated an electron crankcase, wet liners and two separate cylinder heads, the 'cubist' effect mentioned earlier begin further emphasised by the virtual elimination of all external oil ways as the 3½ gallons of working fluid were now contained in the wet sump. The combustion chambers was still of the indirect pattern but the Ricardo concern had been called in as consultant and as a result of its activities, various changes had been made. Despite the alleged updating, there was no exhauster fitted and vacuum was still achieved from the medium of the throttle valve. The size though of the braking reservoir had been increased and sufficient capacity was available to cover up to four power applications.

Crossleys seemed to favour vacuum systems for the fuel was drawn up from the tank by an auto-vacuum and the latter fitting remained right up to the time that the very last chassis came out of Errwood Park.

The chassis frame had been redesigned for the Streamline and now incorporated platform extensions to side members being joined by substantial cross members which were of tubular construction from the rear of the gearbox. Crash boxes were still provided as standard although a constant-mesh unit was offered as an optional extra but this had straight teeth and so still gave rise to the characteristic noise that I have always associated with Crossley transmission. Perhaps the most unusual features of the chassis covered the mounting of the road springs which were severely inclined in elevation to the horizontal, but here experience over Manchester cobbles must have paid off. As I remember things, the standard of ride was good and few springs needed to be replaced in service. There was, though, one suspension detail that did give rise to some problems and I refer here to the front spring rear frame bracket. This both accommodated the shackle pin and an additional spherical bearing reducing twisting stress within the frame member. The accompanying sketch shows clearly the various design

Below: The VR6. The engine shown in this view was a 1939 unit. It retained a very square appearance, now included a dynamo belt driven fan, front engine oil filler, ribbed oil cooler, but still had the induction pipe vent to create braking vacuum.

Right: There can be no doubt that Manchester orders sustained Crossley Motors in the years immediately prior to 1939. Here is one of the 'Streamliner' vehicles, No628, introduced in 1936. Delivery continued until a German air raid damaged the factory leaving some 1938 buses and all 34 of the 1939 order still to come. Other buses in the first batch, 601 and 608-634 had horizontal cream top deck flashes.

features but as will be appreciated extensive wear could, and did, occur with results that ranged from rattles to some odd steering characteristics.

Despite all the foregoing very few examples were to be seen outside Manchester, although that city was still purchasing batches right up to the first year of the war when the Gorton erecting shops were damaged in an air raid, leaving an outstanding balance of about 100 vehicles to be carried over until construction became possible in 1946, and I well remember seeing the first of these together with some distinctive blue South Shields double-deckers running past me as I waited for an older Crossley during the course of delivery, the latter being amongst the very first postwar Crossleys to be built.

The Streamlines obviously went into all day service, unlike Oldham buses which had a rather chequered career. Being none too popular with either the driving or maintenance staffs, they were relegated to peak hour work by 1938 usually running to Shaw Wrens Nest via the level Higginshaw route, but 12 months or so later they completely disappeared and it was not

until much later that I learned they had been on loan to Bristol.

They came back to Oldham in 1942 looking quite new and unmarked to be fitted with new engine parts which brought them on to the direct injection principle and they then returned to full day service featuring on the 4 and V circular routes (later 25 and 26). They were still disliked by most people, but I always regarded No57 with a favourable eye and would ride on it whenever I had the time and a few coppers to spare. Once the war ended scrapping was not long delayed and here we come to a mystery for the only vehicle that had no withdrawal date in its official record was my friend 57; however, the corporation had by then received some new machines and I too was cutting my teeth on some almost identical products, to be dealt with at length a little later, so I failed to notice its absence.

My first professional Crossley encounter was with a 'bomber' and the name was apt if you fully

Left: Postwar chassis. The new DD42 model went into production in 1946 and included the also new Type 7, 525cu in power unit. The frontal appearance and bonnet line was much improved but the radiator continued to bear the familiar Maltese cross symbol. Manchester had 71 of the particular pattern to the 7ft 6in dimension as well as later 8ft 0in wide examples — ordered in batches of 109, then 50 and finally 60 buses to give a postwar Crossley fleet of 290 machines all Crossley-bodied.

Below left: Western Welsh was the only BET company to purchase new Crossley vehicles. Here is 938 with 32-seat Willowbrook coach work to Federation design which entered service in November 1949. The radiator now carries a Crossley nameplate. There were 38 buses in the batch allocated latterly to Crosskeys (13) Pontypool (12) and Bridgend (13) depots.

appreciated that it was the driver who was at the receiving end. It will be realised by now that the Crossley engine in its prewar forms was somewhat suspect, and some places effected a little substitution whenever the chance arose, hence the highly unofficial nomenclature.

I had joined a concern which had managed to lose some VR6 units between 1939 and 1945 and in the place where these had once sat a Gardner 5LW was now to be found. The 'bombers' were retained for odd jobs such as works specials and driving school duties, and as authority had decided that I should obtain a psv badge without delay it was to that establishment that I first reported. An instructor was allocated and he took me for a run around in a new staff car, an experience I fully enjoyed, but stage two was to be rather different.

I was asked to meet him the following lunch hour in the central bus station and there I was shown into the driving seat of a 1937 converted Crossley and told to 'have a go'.

It was the first bus I have ever driven on the open road, not that there was much open about it, as traffic was surprisingly heavy and the bus felt to be not 7ft 6in wide but 70ft. This was bad enough but there were other hazards as well. The locally-mounted engine had no resilient mountings so the noise and vibration had to be experienced to be believed. Then there was that 'new' constant mesh gearbox. If that was easy to change then those on the Condors must have been downright difficult but, as it was fairly well worn, I did manage to 'swop a few cogs' at the appropriate times, but it was not any of these factors that caused me the most worry. It was not only my first bus but also my first-ever centre accelerator. Why this should have been incorporated in the late 1930s I shall never know — perhaps it was just another mark of Crossley originality but it gave me an attack of 'knotted feet'.

After about 10 minutes the novelty of driving that bus had worn right off but other spells followed, all involving 'bombers' until the blessed day came when I passed out on yet another machine of the same type, and it is now a matter of regret that I never did have the chance to drive one of the few that retained their original Crossley engines. Perhaps the reason lay in the fact that as they failed they went out for scrap, and failure would be hastened if they came into unpractised hands. Other Crossleys however were still coming in to join a fleet whose members took several forms all coming within the postwar DD 42 range.

Their progenitor was, of course, the famous Manchester bus No2117 later No2960 (chassis number 92901) that came out of Gorton during the war as an experimental prototype and first introduced the type 7 engine which had a 4½in bore, 5½in stroke and a 525cu in capacity. The compression ration was 15.6:1 and the normal output 100bhp at 1,750rpm. This bus, and certain others, were coupled to a Brockhouse turbo-transmitter which replaced the usual gearbox and gave an easy form of change, but it can be said that the increase of the duty of fuel by 2s 6d (12½p) per gallon which accompanied the end of rationing saw the end of that device irrespective of any other considerations, for the combination did not give economic operation and so the transmitters were invariably replaced by a constant mesh gearbox. Our first batch was basically to the same pattern as No1217 (but had constant mesh boxes) being 7ft 6in wide, but the next lot had been constructed to the new 8ft dimension and so were somewhat heavier and also taxed the engine accordingly.

Now this type had an alloy crankcase which unfortunately tended to go out of alignment in use so that on overhaul it was quite usual to have to remove the crank, refit the bearing caps and then line bore the housings taking as little metal as possible out of the case and whatever else was necessary out of the caps when new bearings could go in, although we always then queried why they had been manufactured from the type of material accepted as standard. The crank, incidentally, was hardened but, not unnaturally, it tended to suffer and so failures were not unknown. Our older hands unanimously agreed, however, that compared to certain earlier Crossleys such troubles were quite insignificant and I should mention here that stories or legends about these machines were legion.

It was said for example that shortly after the first of the Condor series made its appearance the crankshaft broke. Top brass muttered 'unusual', supplied a replacement and asked for the return of the failed component, so that it could be kept in some form of technical museum. Unfortunately, within a very short time all the others could have reposed there with it had the space been available, and here I would refer to a conversation of recent date with a friend who had some 50 or so in his care during the 1942/44 period when he stoutly maintained that the average life for them ran out at 45,000 miles.

Our informants, though, did not cast all their rocks at the motive power department. It was firmly asserted that on another single-deck series parking was always a problem for as passengers went on the handbrake came off. Now this is a possibility if the geometry of the linkage is wrong, but I cannot honestly say that it was, for although I did travel on them it was only as a passenger, and an unsuspecting one at that.

Braking on a postwar Crossley was, however, good. The front brake cams rotated unusually, and against the book, in a counter direction to that of the front wheels when travelling forwards but, nevertheless, stopping was progressive and smooth. The brake drums too did not tend to overheat even when the bus was running on a heavy service and brake adjustment was both simple and straightforward which was more than one could say about some other makes of bus. The rest of the chassis also maintained a high standard and particularly so in respect of the gearbox, springing design, and steering, for these buses had come out before certain dubious improvements, such as the replacement on the front axle races by thrust buttons, had come in. The latter fittings materialised on the next two deliveries which also included synchromesh gearboxes. The drivers accepted the box which was perhaps one of the nicest constant mesh designs ever made — provided you double declutched — but they were loud in voicing their comments regarding the very stiff steering. It must be added that complaints about heavy fuel consumption were also being made although that charge, as can be imagined, came from a rather higher source. Investigation fell to the lot of the technical department which also had some overheating problems on its plate, for immediately the Crossleys were put on to a rather hilly route following a tramway conversion this then dormant propensity made its appearance, but here at least it was possible to find an escape route by returning them to more level pastures. One unusual difficulty occurred when an engine became really hot. Then the valves could come into contact with the cylinder walls and 'scuff' the top of the bores due to expansion of the valve heads taking up the very limited side clearance available.

We really came on to the steering problems in an indirect way. There were some four-wheel trolleybuses which, if anything, were worse than the diesels despite the absence of about a ton of engine weight over the front axle, but far worse even than these was the handful of three-axle trolleys that had interchangeable steering components. We started on these by fitting a new wheel disc that brought the centre of the tyre inwards so that it coincided at ground level with the produced centre line of the kingpin, thus reducing the bending loads on the kingpin bushes, and then did some experiments fitting wedges between the bottom of the front springs and the top of the axle beam in order to alter the castor angle and, as can be imagined, several variations had to be tried before the right characteristics were apparent. The alterations were most successful and instead of a dead and lifeless steering we had some reasonable response to the effort applied and so we moved on to the diesels, but I should add here that it was during this period that I learned something about the cardinal sin of trolleybus driving and this, if you don't know, can be summed up in the following statement. 'Never, but never, overtake the one in front'.

With the diesels we met a snag for most, unlike the trolleybuses, had triple servo vacuum brakes and the different type of wheel disc fouled the front units so these had to be moved inwards on specially-made adaptor plates and this led in turn to some drag line changes. Eventually the fault was cured and in later years the change was applied to buses run by other concerns but I am afraid that we did not have the same success when we came to investigate the fuel consumption difficulties.

We set to work on a number of test buses that first of all had their fuel pumps and injectors properly calibrated and serviced. We then looked at the valve timing and advanced it so that instead of the inlet valve opening about 2½in before top dead centre when measured on the flywheel the dimension became 3½in. Here we came up against certain most interesting valve events that made me realise what troubles a faulty camshaft can bring, but that is quite another story.

Then we tried fitting a cold air induction system and insulating the fuel pump thus giving the engine a denser charge of both air and fuel on the induction and working strokes. This made the unit run at a lower temperature, a fact that was most apparent when we came to do some hilly route tests, but on the debit side better air infiltration was obviously going to be a necessity to reduce cylinder bore wear. All this took quite a time and did not really get to the heart of the

Right: The radiator style changed again for a time in the late 1940s some chassis such as this one being given a chromium plated shell.

matter which was due to poor porting in the initial design.

This fact was realised by the manufacturer which, in March 1950, announced the introduction of a modified type 7 engine (which for some export applications had already been coupled to a supercharger) and this became known as the down draught or 7/5 version. In this design, which showed only a very slight external difference, there being two large air tubes coming over the top of the rocker box, all intake bends had been reduced to a minimum thus bringing the air directly to the valve seats. It was a comparatively small modification although different injector nozzles were also required but it brought the

Above: A Rotherham Crossley of 1951 vintage. The very last Crossley of all HET 513, first licensed by Rotherham on 12 August 1953, was of similar appearance.

power output up to 114bhp again at 1,750rpm at the usual derated figure, although this could be lifted to 136bhp if an operator so desired by simply opening up the fuel pump. This change, along with the reintroduction of a frame mounted five-speed overdrive constant mesh gearbox — shades of the Alpha and Condor — came at a time when the company was selling quite a large number of coach chassis and both figured in a number of such machines, but unfortunately they came too late for, in the writer's view, Crossley suffered yet again from being too early in the field with its postwar design. The 8.6 litre type 7 engine could cope with the prewar size bus but, after about 1948, it could not compare either if life, performance, or returned mpg to the standard set by the 9.6 litre AEC or the 0600 Leyland power units. It was then that something bigger and better should have been offered to the customers, but perhaps there were production difficulties.

As it was the down draught conversion did nothing

to improve bottom end life, but as running and fuel consumption were improved whilst a reduction on exhaust smoke was apparent one could perhaps justify the expenditure of around £110 each involved. Costwise the Crossley chassis was very competitive for a double-deck unit with synchromesh gearbox was being quoted at £1,630 in 1950 whereas Leyland then wanted £1,710 for a similar PD2 and Guy £1,790 for a 6LW-powered Arab with only constant mesh gearing in the case of the latter, but at this stage the company was overtaken by previous policy decisons.

Car manufacture went into a decline after 1930 finally ending towards the end of 1937, one of the last models being the 1½ litre Regis saloon that had a six cylinder Coventry Climax engine and a preselector gearbox. Selling price was then £365, this figure providing a well-finished four-door saloon body. Another factor here was the introduction of the rearmament programme which involved Crossley in the manufacture of substantial goods vehicle orders for the RAF, something which continued until the end of World War II. This was rather odd, as although Crossley had offered civilian goods vehicles with either oil or petrol engines before car construction ceased few were sold afterwards, and no such models reappeared after the war.

Some goods experiment work was done however after 1946 and at least two prototypes were built and then used for works purposes.

By 1946 the company was concentrating entirely on public service vehicles and taking substantial home and overseas orders, one of the latter calling for the virtual re-equipment of the Netherlands bus fleets, and at this time a move was made from the old Gorton factory to other premises at Errwood Park, Stockport, once the scene of Willys-Overland vehicle construction — brand name the Manchester (a company which subsequently amalgamated with Crossley) — but later extended greatly for aircraft manufacturing purposes. The company had also had a factory in Hyde during the war years which was mainly engaged on RAF vehicle work or Mancunian engine rebuilding. It was closed at this time.

For about four years bus production ran at a high level but then the wartime slack was taken up and sales began to fall off and here the idea of putting all the eggs in one basket proved fatal. There is no doubt that, in the mind of the writer, the decline was caused mainly by the shortcomings of the Crossley type 7 engine, down-draught version notwithstanding, but matters cannot have been helped by the lack of any saleable alternative product, plus the failure to make any reasonable impact on the then largest private bus purchasing group.

The last big Crossley contract was the 260-bus Birmingham order and these had Crossley bodies for that department of the company truly did have something that was worth buying, as we found out when our first postwar Crossley bodies came up for re-certification. We had the panels taken off one or two, but there was no corrosion and no sign of any movement so after these preliminary inspections the process was not continued.

The end was inevitable and in 1950 AEC purchased the share capital, largely for the valuable machining facilities the Errwood Park works contained.

At first there seemed to be some chance the Crossley chassis would continue with AEC power units (although I have been told that a bigger Crossley engine was on the drawing board) but in a short time 'badge engineering' for commercial shows became the order of the day. Then followed a brief rise in Crossley fortunes during the time the integral ACV Group Bridgemaster was under development, but that soon ceased, and completion of the 62 BUT trolleybus chassis for Manchester, (another AEC design, few postwar Crossley trolleybuses being built) marked the end of new chassis construction.

Bodybuilding continued for another year or two but then the comet was burned right out and the factory gates closed for the last time in 1958 when one or two staff members were still coming to work in well preserved Regis saloon motorcars. The very last Crossley to be completed was chassis number 95908 which left Rotherham after receiving a Crossley body in the August of 1953 to become No213, although its sister No214 which had an earlier chassis number was the last of all to be registered. It took the road one month later.

Fortunately, one or two examples including No213 and ex-Oldham No368 have been preserved and at a rally a year or two ago I was given the chance to take the wheel again and so experience that nostalgic Crossley feel.

It only needed a mile of travel to remind me just how good that postwar Crossley might have been, for the standard of ride, driver visibility, and general chassis engineering were of the highest order, but all the excellence was masked by that all too familiar woolly engine note. Nevertheless, the absence of that same sound was noted with regret when I last paid one of my now infrequent visits to Manchester.

I still have a soft spot for the make and regret that the firm did not manage to survive as an independent into this age of the giants. If it had, then by now Errwood Park could have been turning out a 10 litre rear-engined integral double-decker and it might even have been called 'The Gortonian'. That author, as it happended, was never to have another Crossley fail at his gate, but not too long after that event a rather different machine took his eye — a machine that was built on to very firm foundations.

6
Firm Foundation –Bristol Fashion

One morning in the spring of 1936 I was waiting for the bus to school at my usual stop and filling in what would otherwise have been some wasted waiting minutes by interesting myself in the activity going on over the pavement wall.

The bus route at this particular location followed a loop round three sides of a small terminal railway station whose perimeter was marked by the aforementioned masonry but the highway on the far side was some 30 feet below the spot on which I was standing and the difference in level was made up along the short piece of road that ran parallel to the buffer stops and possessed quite a gradient as a consequence. The gradient was in fact sufficient to change the tone of the Tilling tinkle from soprano to bass, only this morning there was no tinkle.

Instead my ears were filled with a veritable roar which was quite sufficient to drown the snorting of the Webb coal tank engine whose arrival with the branch line train had attracted my interest, but my gaze soon left that piece of Victorian engineering when the cause of the noise came into view for the culprit was a brand new Bristol single-decker.

Now Bristols at that time were rather rare in the Greater Manchester area although that same city's tramway department had purchased a number in earlier years, but the 26 operating survivors no longer came into my orbit (the last was withdrawn finally in 1937) and my recollections of them were distinctly hazy, although in actual fact an A type converted to a crane truck lasted until 1954. From this moment onwards, however, Bristol buses became quite a feature of local life and when on considers the service they gave to their owner it must be admitted that someone somewhere (Stockport perhaps?) had made a very wise choice.

This second generation of Manchester District Bristols did, though, have a Gardner engine as the propulsion unit and, as the Bristol/Gardner combination became a byword for the acme of

reliability both of the firms of reliability both of the firms and their products they deserve a very special mention here.

The chassis manufacturing half of the partnership has origins which date back to 1870, for in that year an attempt was made by a group of financiers to lay tramway tracks in the City of Bristol. This suggestion met with opposition from the municipality that then obtained powers to carry out the work itself and this was commenced in 1873. Unfortunately the enabling act did not allow the corporation to act as a tramway operator as well as owner but eventually some local men formed a company for the purpose that began to work the first route with horse traction on the 9 August 1875.

The Bristol Tramways Company, as the new concern was called, traded successfully and in 1887 took part in a merger when it combined with the Bristol Cab Co and so came to add the unusual words 'and carriage' to its original tramways title. Even more unusually perhaps it engaged in the business of funeral undertaking, and here is a thought for anyone wishing to revive an ailing 1978/9 style bus company.

Horses, of course, continued to provide the motive power for these activities (although steam traction was tried, but unsuccessfully so for a short period) until 1895 when one of the tramway routes was altered to electric working and by 1900 the whole system had been similarly converted, a process which rendered about 800 animals redundant, although some were used to power the 30 horsebus routes opened in the latter year.

Motorbus operation was inaugurated as early as January 1906 and one month later three more routes were added, only the latter were noteworthy in that they ran beyond the boundaries of the city. These services were worked by vehicles of Thornycroft manufacture but after obtaining very valuable operating experience the company decided to carry out some experimental construction on its own account, and so in 1908 the first home-made machine was put into use after completion at Filton.

The type was multiplied and by 1912 progress was sufficiently good to warrant the setting up of a manufacturing unit at Brislington which became known as the Motor Constructional Works, and with these new premises came a new machine, the 4-ton model with a 48bhp four-cylinder engine. Buses of this type were built for the next two years but then World War I came and the Brislington shops turned over to aircraft construction for the duration.

This unwarranted interruption lasted for some four years but a certain amount of design and development work was undertaken within this period with a prototype chassis being produced in 1915 which had a Bristol AW type engine. Consequently, as soon as it was possible to do so, serious production began, actually in 1920, of an improved 4-tonner based on this last vehicle which had a large 60bhp engine BW power unit and of course normal control.

Like most chassis of its time it was suitable for use as either a goods or passenger carrier and in order to boost sales which eventually exceeded the 700 mark a

Below left: Riding in the cab of this early specimen No13 in the Bristol fleet must have been a draughty business. The arched doorways verge on the Gothic.

Below: A 1922 32-seat 4ton normal-control type as purchased by Doncaster Corporation which was a Bristol customer for over 20 years.

Above: Nearby Rotherham put this front-entrance 2ton forward-control model into service one year later. The exact fare notice has a modern air. This undertaking too became a firm Bristol fan.

stand was taken at the 1921 Commercial Vehicle Show which meant that the Bristol was now available on a national basis.

A much lighter 2-tonner followed in 1923 which was another dual purpose chassis incorporating the forward control layout, a full width front and came complete with pneumatic tyres. The four-cylinder petrol engine of Bristol manufacture that provided the motive power was of the smaller 48bhp 1,850rpm form. Incidentally the forward control layout was a unique feature that was not too be repeated for a considerable number of years.

This model was quite successful but another heavy duty machine known as the A type followed in 1925 which had a low loading chassis frame and was designed to accommodate either double- or single-deck bodies. As a result a still larger 80bhp 2,000rpm six cylinder engine (type reference FW) was included but for some reason the design was none too successful and only 18 double-deckers and 4 single-deckers were produced between 1926 and 1928 with one other chassis becoming a horsebox, but any ground lost here was more than recovered by its famous successor the B type.

The B was first produced in 1926 and 778 were built before construction finally came to an end, a process incidentally which must have placed a considerable strain on the Brislington premises as virtually every part was made therein including the petrol tank, radiator and, very unusually, the propeller shaft universal joints. Other noteworthy features were the GW type engine giving 75bhp at 2,000rpm with a bore of 4¾in and a 6in stroke, an underslung worm drive offset rear axle, and a low chassis weight of 2 tons 6cwt.

Many chassis received Bristol-built bodies, the company referring to the completed vehicle as the 'Superbus' and it certainly attracted some substantial interest, for in 1928 and 1929 by way of example orders came in not only from other companies but also from the municipalities of Aberdeen (3), Merthyr (2), Rotherham (21), Exeter (2), Doncaster (10), West Harlepool (4), Manchester (12), Hull (6), Wigan (4), Bradford (14), Cardiff (4), St Helens (2) and Aberdeen (1). An impressive list!

From the B came several variations. The D type had a 6-cylinder 4in bore, 6in stroke, JW engine and just 50 were built. Of these 41 went into the Bristol fleet the other nine being split between Rhondda (6) Greyhound (2) and Graham, of Kirkintilloch (1).

Another B type variant was the J type model which was introduced in 1932 and which incorporated the 4in by 6in JW engine that had been used initially in the 50D type chassis mentioned above. In 1933, however, J series chassis number 127 was given a 4-cylindered LW engine, re-classified as chassis number H101 and so formed the prototype of yet another range. The story though, is by no means ended, for in 1934 the J type came to be offered also with a four-cylindered engine reference NW and, in order to show clearly what had what the alternative chassis references JJW and JNW came to be employed.

Then there was the double-deck version with suitably-stiffened components designated the G type which also had as standard the petrol six-cylinder engine; but changes were now in the air for on 14 April 1933 a Gardner 5LW engine number 30353 left Patricroft en route for Brislington.

Lawrence Gardner the founder of the firm which bears his name commenced in business as a metal machinist in 1868 in a workshop formed from the cellars that lay beneath four cottages in Duke Street, Manchester. The business slowly prospered and after taking out a building society loan he purchased the premises, but by the time the debt had been cleared output was sufficient to justify the erection of a brand new building in nearby Cornbrook Park Road. Lawrence was sadly not able to see much further development as he died at an early age in 1890 leaving the firm to his widow and children (six sons and two daughters), the boys fortunately possessing the inventive genius of their father, the two eldest being the first ever Whitworth Scholars.

In 1891 another move was made for the firm, now known as L. Gardner and Sons, was employing about 80 people and making a variety of products, perhaps the most unusual of these being a range of dentist's chairs. The year of the move, though, saw construction of a small hot air engine and in 1894 the first Gardner gas engine was built to sell for £12.10.

Four short years later the still new Lund Street factory was again too small for requirements and the move to Barton Hall works was made where sufficient space was available for future development, although the proprietors could never have imagined at the time just how the company would expand in the next 30 years.

Gardners was now specialising in internal combustion engines and taking an interest in both the stationary and marine markets and it was through the latter that the break into the automative world really came.

About 1925 Joseph Gardner, one of the younger sons began to develop a new series of diesel engines and his first approach was to investigate the two stroke principle, but this was discarded in a fairly short time with the result that 1928 saw the making of the worlds first small high speed open chamber (or direct injection) four stroke engine with what are now conventional multi-holed injectors, an engine which was first shown in public at the August 1929 Shipping and Machinery Exhibition under the type reference L2. The very first engine (number 28203) had four cylinders hence the designation 4L2, a bore of 4¼in a 6in stroke, a 5.6 litre capacity and an output of 38bhp at 1,000rpm. It was, as has been implied, intended for marine work and so the layout was arranged accordingly, for a ship's engine is mounted well down in the vessel's hull and thus any necessary maintenance work has to be done from the top. As a result the crankcase was split on the bearing centre line, and this and all the other major non-rotating parts were of cast iron.

This engine and the larger six-cylinder unit which followed had a specific fuel consumption which was phenomenal by the standards of the day and still as good as average in 1978. It came on the market when the bus industry was beginning to look seriously for an alternative to the expensive petrol engine, for the rate of fuel usage mentioned in the Crossley chapter was by no means peculiar to that particular make and it must be remembered here that diesel oil which cost only 4d per gallon was not subject to tax at that time.

As it happened Gardners took just three 4L2 orders during the period of the show, engines numbered 28421 and 28422 being subsequently produced for marine generating sets, but the third which formed the reason for the existence of unit number 28423 came from a very different business.

One very interested visitor had been Trevor Barton of the Barton bus concern who had come away so convinced as to the possibilities offered by this new Gardner product that he had signed the necessary form and so on 28 February 1930 his 4L2 engine left the Gardner despatch bay being consigned to the company's Beeston Nottingham depot, and there it was installed in a Lancia single-deck bus replacing the original petrol unit.

A short testing period followed for crankshaft speed had been raised to give an output of 50bhp at 1,300rpm and then in March the vehicle was returned

Left: The 1926 A type double-decker of fearsome aspect in the process of being tilt tested. Tyre deflection should not have given rise to much variation in the position of the centre of gravity.

Above: One of the last B type buses to be built was this single-decker which also entered the Doncaster fleet in 1930.

to normal service and perhaps much more, for in less than 12 months 50,000 miles had been run and at that point the engine was removed and returned to Patricroft for examination. The amount of wear was virtually negligible and so 28423 was sold again this time on 29 Febuary 1931 to another customer, Northern Motor Utilities, a haulier, and thus vanishes from this story.

In the meantime in June 1930 the fifteenth such engine had passed into the hands of Messrs Dutsons of Leeds which fitted it to a Leyland lorry and so was able to offer the first British commercial oil engined conversion for sale to the goods side of the road transport industry, but larger and basically simpler engines were also being produced by this time.

The 6L2 came next, the pioneer engine 28463 being finished on 31 March to begin life in a yacht at the marine rating of 58bhp; then followed the intermediate 5L2 version which commenced with engine number 28506 that was passed off test on 29 April 1930, although at first sight the building of an engine with five cylinders seems to be an odd sort of task to undertake.

Both types of engine went into automotive duty, Bartons taking a 5L2 in June, its unit number 28509 being set to develop 62bhp, rather less than that of the ninth 6L2 number 28686 set to 75bhp which was purchased by Leeds City Transport on 21 August to appear later in the Crossley double-deck vehicle as already noted. Here there was an interesting pioneering connection as the works manager of Dutsons, Mr T. H. Parkinson, who had been largely responsible for the Leyland conversion and in fact drove the vehicle on its first run, had by now become involved in the Crossley alterations and was later to hold the appointment as motor vehicle rolling stock superintendent, and then chief engineer to the Leeds transport undertaking.

Two other early 6L2s went as conversions into Crossley double-deckers, the thirteenth going to Sheffield Corporation and the eighteenth number 28778 to Manchester, the latter sale being dated 17 October 1930, but the manufacturing side of the industry was also displaying an interest with Karrier Motors being an early customer putting engine number 12 into a goods chassis.

By the end of 1932 about 200 L2 engines had entered automotive service and perhaps the smallest of these was the 3L2, actually the first of the three-cylinder version to be produced, which was put to

Above: A Gardner SL2 engine ready for a marine installation. The substantial construction employed is clearly seen.

Right: One of the early 5LW units. Note the alloy crankcase, front mounted exhauster, fuel pump still with priming levers and the rubber hose dynamo shaft coupling.

work powering a Wallis and Stevens road roller, but by then the day of this type of unit was done in so far as road traction was concerned for a much more suitable version was quickly made available, and again it came at a most opportune time.

Between 1930 and 1933 certain wellknown legislation came into effect which had a profound effect on the carriage of goods or passengers by road, but the part of the Traffic Acts with which we are concerned here is that which restricted vehicle weights and dimensions, for the former stressed the need for a high engine power/weight ratio and so the new Gardner LW range really came into its own.

Gardners wisely in developing this series took the best of the L2 design and so many vital dimensions, like bore and stroke, remained unchanged, as did other important fuel injection, combustion chamber and bearing characteristics, but the crankshaft was now housed in an alloy case of the conventional automobile layout so that the bearing could be reached once the sump had been removed, and of course access was possible from the underside.

The prototype engine 6LW 29150, completed in June 1931, was utilised for a number of years in the experimental department and finally ended its days as a static exhibit in the firm's London showrooms in rather marked contrast to its earlier relation the first 4L2. That engine is still to be found hard at work in the Barton Hall Works power house, but this aspect of long life was to become just as apparent in the LWs even though they were designed to run at a maximum crank shaft speed of 1,700rpm.

The first production 6LW number 29240 went to Karrier on the 26 October 1931 and the next three to Scammell, Guy and Tilling Stevens respectively for incorporation in goods vehicle chassis, but here we come to the new restrictions on vehicle sizes, for if length was now firmly fixed by law it followed that the

Above: The first Gardner engined J05G1 with Bristol rear entrance body.

longer the engine the shorter must be the passenger space behind the bulkhead.

As most buses were single-decked and only carried about 32 people the 102bhp of the lengthy 6LW was rather on the generous side and so a replacement for the 5L2 was going to be useful. Thus was born the first 5LW. As engine number 29269 it was despatched on 5 November 1931 to the London General Omnibus Company which fitted it into an AEC CC type chassis and carried out some prolonged testing. The engine was set to give 85bhp at 1,700rpm and like its predecessors was to have a long life for after return from London for examination after the usual high mileage build up it went to power a works truck, but, by the time it was back in Lancashire, 5LWs were to be found in many buses. The first to be used this way in a production sense was sister unit 29885, the fortieth to be built, that went into a Daimler single-deck chassis, was subsequently exported to the wellknown city of Las Palmas, and could be there yet still in full use.

It will be noted from all this that the Bristol company was about 18 months behind some of its competitors but from April 1933 onwards development was rapid.

It all began with the arrival at Bristol of that 5LW engine, a unit set to deliver 80bhp at the usual 1,700rpm and this was then fitted into the existing prototype chassis number H101 thus displacing the LW 4-cylinder petrol engine of Brislington manufacture that had originally been installed as mentioned earlier. The resulting oil engined assembly was given the new identity J05G1, as the reproduction of the original specification sheet clearly shows, and then put into the bodyshops where a Bristol 36-seat rear-entrance body was fitted. On completion it undertook demonstration duties until 1 February 1936 when it entered the associated Bristol service fleet as number JOG 1, but here it is pertinent to mention that the original registration number AHW 393 that was issued to it in June 1934 was retained.

It might have been the first of the line but its subsequent career provided sufficient proof as to the soundness of the J05G design for in 1943 No2000, as it was known from 1937, was given a new body with the slightly larger capacity of 37 seats, built to wartime standards, and returned to traffic. It continued until the last day of 1954 when withdrawal finally took place, but now comes the mystery for it was purchased by the South Wales Motor Traders concern to vanish completely, but it may yet be serving some remote community as the latter company exported a large number of complete buses around 1955 and so J05G1 could well have formed a part of consignments sent to Cyprus, or beyond.

It will have been noted here that quite a time elapsed between the completion of the first GOG bus and its entry into regular passenger service, and as a result this honour went to J15G2. That also received a Bristol-built body, this time of the 32-seat coach type that surprisingly passed right outside the company orbit for it was purchased by the firm of A&R Graham, Kirkintilloch. Entering service as fleet number 28 (SN 6309) on 19 May 1934 it too, was to have a long passenger-carrying career, until after passing through at least four hands and being given a new Smith 35-seat coach body in 1949 it was finally

THE BRISTOL TRAMWAYS & CARRIAGE COMPANY LTD. — MOTOR CONSTRUCTIONAL WORKS.

Delivered—Chassis only		Weight	Front Axle	Rear Axle	Total	Renumbered J.O.5G-1. STOCK No. ~~H.101.~~	5
,, With Body		Chassis Only With 30 gal Tank.	2. 5. 3.13	1.16. 2.21	4. 2. 2. 6	Sanction No.	1
Type of Body	Demonstration Bus with Gardner Engine. 1933 Show.	With Body	3. 4. 0. 14	2. 14. 3. 14	6. 19. 0. 0	Series No. AHW. 393 6/6/34	34

CUSTOMER B. T. & C. C. L. 30/1/36 — Body Builders Tram Depot.

ENGINE	Gardner LW-5. Cushion Mounted. N° 30353
Conn. Rods	Engine Reconditioned by Gardner. Feb 1935
Carburettor	
Magneto	
Fan	Not fitted.
Pistons	
Cylinder Head	
Oil Filter	
Petrol Filter	Zenith, Plate Type.
GEAR BOX	~~GB-121~~. KB.101 4/12/33
CLUTCH	K.N. To 3 RN Drawing.
	Special Shaft for Gardner Engine. 16 KN.
FRONT AXLE	GE-129.
Springs	159/160 GE. Shackled.
REAR AXLE	~~JM-323~~. 463 21/8/34
Ratio	~~5.2/5~~: 1. 6:1
Springs	204/5 JM. Shackled.
Prop. Shaft	Hardy Spicer.
TYRES	30 x 9.00 L.P.Dunlop.
BRAKES	Single Shoe. Twin Gear.
Servo	Dewandre with Vacuum Cylinder.
CHANGE SPEED	Special Bracket for Gardner Engine.

RADIATOR	J.V. Special Connections, no Fan Tunnel.
PETROL TANK	Shortened. 30 Gal.
Autovac	AV 43.
LIGHTING	F.L.
Dynamo	CAV.D-76. 12v.
Batteries	Exide Ironclad. BMV-5.
Switchboard	CAV. 54-B-7.
Control Board	" 37-C-21.
Lamps—Head	CRBF.60.S/G.
,, Side	RC 440.
,, Tail	Stop Light.
BULKHEAD	Special XJ.
BONNET	Standard GJ.
STEERING	JG-Bristol. (26th Sanction).
FRAME & Wheelbase	XA. 17'6".
SPEEDOMETER	Smith's 60 mph.
OUTRIGGERS	
HORNS	Lucas Electric & Bulb.
LUBRICATION	Zerk Group.

purchased by a dealer who converted it into a goods vehicle and then resold it for still further service in its new role.

It is not surprising that the J05G became a best seller, no less than 562 being built up to 1937, if one exclused the solitary AEC-engined version J06A2, when the model was superseded by the L5G, a fate that was then suffered by the companion G05G intended for double-deck bodywork that must also be given a brief mention. This corresponding chassis designation became the K5G.

Two of the aforementioned G type chassis numbers 123 and 124 also had their JW petrol engines extracted and two 5LWs fitted instead, Brush 52-seat lowbridge bodywork was added, and both then went into service in 1934 as part of the Keighley/West Yorkshire fleet as chassis numbers G05G1 and G05G2. Three other chassis originally Nos G122, G128 and GJW 139 appeared in chassis intended for the Aberdare and Pontypridd municipalities, but only five were included in the final total of 277 Bristol double-deckers that had been constructed by 1937, when the K and L types reached the production stage, although other variations must be noted as 16 single-deckers received 6LW engnes and entered Black & White coach stock in 1936 and 1937 as J06Gs whilst 14J06 As took AEC engines and a further 13 the

Above: Reproduction of the manufacturers record sheet for chassis JO5G1 which shows how the identity was changed from H101.

Above right: North Western L type Bristol 31-seater No916, one of the 1938 batch, posed in Lower Mosely Street, Manchester Bus Station when new. Note the side destination board, then a normal fitting.

Dennis four-cylinder unit thus becoming type J04D. Still later experiments saw the use of Beardmore and Leyland engines in chassis G125 and G05G 116 respectively, the former having a very short life.

It is interesting to speculate what might have happened if the Gardner had not been so good, for the Bristol company did not immediately abandon all petrol engine development. Five improved standard units, three type MW and two type PW, were built and used in about three different chassis but much more important work continued through 1934/5 on the revolutionary Redrup Wobble plate engine that had two forms employing rotary or poppet valves respectively. This unit was of circular construction and instead of a conventional crankshaft had a plain central shaft which carried a circular disc mounted at an angle. The piston rods bore on to the disc so that as it turned fore and aft movement was imparted to the rods and pistons, with the net result that on the firing stroke pressure was applied to the disc which then turned until the piston was returned to the top of the cylinder after the following exhaust movement when the cycle began all over again. It will be appreciated here that the nine-cylinder construction should have provided a very smooth running unit, but technical difficulties were considerable. Although one was shown at the 1935 Show and another run on service in Manchester of all places the idea was abandoned largely because the Bristol company passed at this time into the hands of the Tilling group which had resolved to pin its faith on the diesel engine. Apparently four such engines were built, RR1 (poppet valves) going into the 1933 J type show chassis which was then reclassified JAX 1. The chassis received a 32-seat front-entrance body and ran in Bristol from 1 August 1935 until 12 September 1935 when it went

Left: A Willowbrook postwar rebody of one of the North Western K5Gs.

Below left: The nearside rear view of a Bristol AVW engine showing layout of the manifolds and auxiliaries and the long dipstick tube which must have made access very easy.

on to demonstration duty but subsequent history is decidedly vague, although it is on record that the bus was later dismantled after extensive damage following a clutch explosion.

Memories of this unique venture are now rather dimmed by the passage of time, but one of my still active colleagues was associated with some experimental use and I asked him what went wrong with it. His reply consisted of the single word 'everything'.

It was the new Tilling management that was responsible for the introduction of the L and K types, these provided worthy successors to the Tilling Stevens machines that had for so long been the main stay of many associated fleets, and it was, of course, through this new connection that I came to meet my first Bristol vehicle, actually a J05G in the fleet number series 727 to 750 inclusive, at my station bus stop.

It slowed to a halt giving me time to cast an eye over the imposing radiator with its polished aluminium surround and neat Bristol nameplate before it came my turn to pass through the rear door and into the saloon furnished to full North Western standards. We had high-backed moquette-trimmed seats, neat totally-enclosed light fittings on the grained and varnished pillars, maroon curtains, and a moquette-covered bulkhead which had a projection in the middle through which sprouted a cast aluminium wheel some 6in in diameter bearing the legend 'heat on — heat off' and corresponding arrows to indicate the necessary direction of rotation.

We settled down on the cushions, the driver revved up, sharp vibrations passed through the vehicle, there was a roar from the rear and off we went. The noise dropped off as second gear was engaged with a rasp and the process was then repeated for third and top. This, though, was not the end of the procedure for the driver ran it up to about 30, took his foot off the accelerator, worked the gear lever, a substantial metallic 'clonk' was heard and then we streaked away in overdrive almost silently and passed everything else on the road until the next village was reached when it all began again. We arrived at school, I recall, rather early and from that time on until the start of the war we had some most exhilarating trips and the old Tilling Stevens machines, sad to say, became objects for derision whenever they appeared on occasions which became ever less frequent. This first batch was followed in October 1936 by Nos774 to 803 which gave North Western a total of 54 J05G vehicles.

Our route was worked apart from two rush hour trips per day by single-deckers (L type chassis appearing in 1938 as No828 to 877 and 899 to 843) right up to 1939, but then to offset a reduction in frequency designed to save fuel etc double-deckers were allocated to the workings. So we came to know the 64 corresponding North Western K types, 816 to 827 and 884-895 of 1938 vintage or 944-983 that came out in that last year of peace.

These were built to the same standard of comfort as

the single-deckers and even the four-in-one upper sallon lowbridge pattern seats had high backs. They made sightseeing even more difficult than usual on a bus of this arrangement but my how those vehicles could motor! They also worked on the express route into Manchester that had only a few stops along a descending section of about five miles and I often think now it was a pity that someone of the calibre of C. J. Allen or O. S. Nock could not have produced a series of articles on bus practice and performance around Greater Manchester during this period. If they had there can be no doubt as to which vehicle would have held the speed record and it wouldn't have been a Crossley, although conversely they could well have had some pungent things to say about Bristol hill-pulling powers and the teethsetting vibrations that followed the moment any adverse gradient was encountered that called for the selection of third or second gears.

The L and K chassis were of almost identical construction, employing similar running units, the major difference being in the wheelbase of 17ft 6in and 16ft 3in although the five-speed overdrive constant mesh gearbox was standard in the L type, the double-decker having a basically similar four-speed assembly.

Regrettably I have no direct maintenance experience with this generation of Bristol but fortunately I knew someone who had, so I went along to ask the usual questions. My acquaintance called over his assistant and the two put their heads together, thought for a bit, and then one said 'Well we did have to adjust the clutches fairly often didn't we?' His colleague agreed and that was that!

You might think that such a reply denoted either a complete lack of interest or a pair of failing memories and I must admit to one or two suspicisions, but in any event such answers were not going to help this narrative along so I went elsewhere and looked up two more gentlemen, one now a retired chief engineer the other the present holder of that situation and previously his assistant, who were well versed in running Bristols.

They didn't think at all, both being certain that here was too much braking effort on the rear wheels and not enough on the front. 'What else? I asked. The reply I received was to the effect that they were a robust and unsophisticated chassis that had no definite faults. At this stage the elder of the two mentioned that he started his career with the Karrier company, and the statement I made in Chapter 4 was immediately proved true. We touched on three-axled problems and then I was regaled with a fascinating account of what it was like to build a sleeve valve engine for a double-decker of that type, under workshop conditions of 1927 vintage.

Bristols, though, retained some engine aspirations after the wobble plate concept was laid to rest and these took a tangible form in 1938 when the design of an oil engine was initiated. This was intended specifically to provide a six-cylinder alternative for the then standard 5LW and so the general arrangement was subjected right from the start to a restriction on length that was to effect the entire concept. A single cylinder test unit was built and from this came a 110mm bore 143mm stroke direct injection 8.15 litre engine governed to procuce 100bhp at 1,700rpm. Four experimental prototypes were made and distributed around the Tilling Group for service testing under the type reference XOW, and the first of these could have been working in chassis number 45136 as early as March 1939, but the war was to prevent further activity for some considerable time.

Eventually in the August of 1946 VW engine No101 was produced to be followed by 11 more until No112 was completed in May 1947, and after these pre-production units came the main stream for inclusion as a Gardner alternative in the K and L type chassis that had been updated to the basic designs they were to follow for the next decade.

The layout was designed to give a straight transmission line from the engine to the rear axle, and could accommodate one of the four alternative power units then being fitted, these being the AEC 7.7 unit, the Gardner 5 or 6-cylinder alternatives and of course the AVW.

This retained the 8.15 litre capacity and the bore and stroke dimensions mentioned above. The iron alloy cylinder block had six dry liners and these were covered by two heads cast from the same material as the block. The induction system was the subject of a Bristol patent specially intended to give a high air velocity through venturi tubes shaped to impart a swirl past the valve seatings. The crankshaft, stiffly webbed, was carried in seven lead bronze/white metal bearings and had 3⅝in diameter crank pin journals, whilst steel shell bearings were used in the big ends of the substantial connecting rods. Rather surprisingly a triple row timing chain was employed instead of the more postive gear chain, but one good point was the provision of an oil filter at the front of the 4½in gallon well-ribbed cast aluminium sump which could be drained and cleaned without having to disturb the lubricant in the dropped reservoir portion.

Behind the engine was a 17in diameter clutch with a flexible lining, particular attentioin having been paid to ease of adjustment of the renewal of any working parts. A five-speed gearbox was now standard with a constant mesh third and overdrive, the latter consisting of pair of gears mounted at the front of the assembly (although a four ratio unit could still be obtained) and then at the end of the line was a worm drive assembly having 8in centres.

The rest of the chassis with its new style radiator, low bonnet line, 11in deep frame, and 3½in wide springs was generously proportioned as were the brake lining areas, for front and rear shoes having widths of 3½in or 7½in were contained in drums having a diameter of 17in or slightly above that figure. The brakes too retained that excellent Bristol feature which allowed individual adjustment of the shoes to be made via the medium of a detachable key.

The end result was a sound vehicle devoid of any frills and it must here be mentioned that before the drawings were passed for production a committee of leading Tilling engineers was given the opportunity of reviewing all facets of the intended design.

In some respects the first postwar Bristol was perhaps just a little too simple, for I well remember a three-hour ride taken one hot summer evening on the lower deck nearside front seat of a K type double-decker complete with 5LW engine that would have been much kinder to the senses if only flexible engine mountings had been provided plus a little better power/weight ratio, but the AVW versions were certainly better in this respect, although, within the garage, opinion seemed to favour the Gardner.

My second set of friends said that around 1950 their 40 odd AVWs were being docked at intervals of 25,000 miles and required a complete overhaul at about 150,000 miles thus falling short of the 200,00 figure achieved by the Gardners, although one must add in all fairness that most of the latter engines were in single-deckers whilst every double-decker had an AVW. One weak spot was the white metal portion of the main bearings that would crack as a result of metal fatigue and then fail, but timing chain and the adjusting sprockets also needed fairly careful watching.

They then turned up some old record cards that showed, on a 44,000 mile per annum life, fuel and lubricating oil consumption figures of 9.1 and 9.40mpg which must be regarded as very satisfactory and once again they did not have a bad word to say about the chassis. In fact at this stage mention was made of a competitive make of vehicle tried next which consumed fuel at the rate of 8.2mpg plus mechanics' times on an ever greater percentage increase.

Unfortunately changing traffic trends eventually brought an end to the production of these excellent buses. The last batch of L type single-deckers (15 chassis for Wilts and Dorset) was turned out in 1954, two years after batch production ceased, being replaced by the LS range of underfloor engined chassis some of which possessed the AVW power unit suitably modified to run in a horizontal plane and known as the LSW. The K type double-decker lasted for another three years until late in 1957 when chassis number 118045 received an Eastern Coach Works body and entered Brighton Hove and District service as fleet number 500, registration number MPM 500.

Above left: Postwar product. A K6A of 1949 in Maidstone & District service. Weymann bodywork on Bristol chassis was very rare.

Above: Rebodied Bristol. One of the many prewar chassis to receive this treatment taken alongside the last to go into service with the Bristol operating company.

The Bristol operating company had placed its last example in stock a little earlier on 1 October 1957 (fleet number C8431) at a time when its very first such bus C3082 was still running, although this 20-year old veteran which was finally withdrawn on 30 November 1957 had been rebodied in 1949 and fitted with the postwar radiator and low line bonnet assembly.

The replacement for the K was the 27ft long Lodekka, but there was nothing hasty about this process for well over 1,500 of this later chassis had been constructed before the final demise of the K. The Lodekka was the subject of some modification around this time for six 30ft long 70-seat experimental units had been built, and the new single-deck chassis the MW was also on the point of entering full production.

It was obvious that bigger buses which would require bigger engines were coming into fashion and so the AVW engine was also updated. The new BVW version was fitted with a different cylinder block which accommodated wet liners, and these had their bores increased by 5mm to 115mm so that capacity rose to 8.90 litres and power output to 105bhp at 1,600rpm. Other desirable improvements were the incorporation of an all geared timing drive and precision shell main bearings.

In this form it was to continue until March 1958 when still higher power outputs became necessary and so the firm began to standardise mainly on the Gardner 6LX or Leyland motive power. Totals of 12 VW, 2,828 AVW, 1,343 BVW and 148 LSW Bristol oil engines were produced in the 12-year production run.

This change severed the link with the prewar and early postwar chassis, and whilst the later Brislington products have clearly indicated the continuing ability of Bristol technicians to produce outstanding products, their histories and characters are right outside the scope of these pages.

The K and L types though which came to number 4,147 and 3,291 respectively must be ranked amongst the 'greats' of the bus world and if any enthusiast should doubt this statement then let him carry out a very simple test. Answer the question 'What type of chassis has been rebodied more than any other?' There is but one answer and as bus undertakings never lightly discard profit-making assets a single conclusion remains. Truly any bus of this era built on to a Bristol chassis was based on very firm foundations.

7

Postwar Romps with AEC Regents

One of the tasks I most detested as a schoolboy was that of having to run errands so it was in a rather cross frame of mind that I entered a shop in close proximity to my then new home in the early months of the last war. The proprietor himself was behind the counter that morning and perhaps because he had time to spare and was curious he asked me a few questions about my interests. On learning that I was attracted towards transport he asked if I would like a book on buses and so I came to possess my first ever copy of a trade journal plus the promise of more to follow.

After that I quite looked forwards to one shopping excursion when true to his word the copy for the current month would be passed over and this usually would be still secured in its original wrapper. I learned a good deal from those magazines, in fact I read them from cover to cover, and even the personality pages were of interest for it was from them that I came to discover what such giants of the industry as R. Stuart Pilcher, J. W. Womar, and E. H. Edwardes looked like, together with the surprising fact that my donor friend was the chairman of the local municpal bus undertaking.

Some issues though had their disappointments and the very first had quite the biggest. The interior was largely given up to the description of the first AEC Regent III to enter provincial service an event that occurred in Glasgow on the 26 March 1940 when bus No723 took the road but perhaps my attitude was excusable as I had not then seen a Glasgow bus and in any event Regents were not very numerous within the greater Manchester area. Salford, Bury, and Rochdale had a few but none seemed to run as smoothly as a Leyland or have the unique character of a Crossley, so after quickly leafing through the pages allocated to this newcomer I dismissed the whole lot as inconsequential and here I apologise to the Regent III for that very wrong assunption.

Now in later years I was to find myself involved with the running of a batch of pre-1939 AEC buses and there was no doubt that they were a most reliable bunch, but not even the aftermath of hard wartime service could disguise the fact that they were unpolished diamonds. They all had the 8.8 engine which seemed to 'thrash' along, and most also possessed preselector gearboxes with a change speed lever that sprouted from the floor and gear pedals that really required two feet to operate them successfully. I say successfully because those pedals had metal pads with an angled foot retainer. Failure to make a complete stroke usually meant that the pedal would fly right back when the retainer and ankle bone would come into violent contact.

There were also sundry other defects such as dubious engine mountings, none too reliable timing chains and chain adjusters, and in vehicles with 7.7 litre engines a power output that was rather on the low side, but no such complaints could be levied against the Regent Mark III which at the time No723 took the road was year ahead of its time.

It all originated with the desire of the then London Passenger Transport Board to obtain a vehicle that could cope with traffic conditions in the capital which even in those far off days were decidedly difficult.

The protype chassis went into use in the latter part of 1938 with a secondhand body, when stringent testing was undertaken. When it was apparent that the conception was basically correct, new coachwork was

Above right: The first Regent. The progenitor of the breed. MT 2114 when new, this bus was later sold to Halifax Corporation which then adopted the orange, green, cream Glasgow livery in which it was painted for its first demonstration run.

Right: Prewar Regent. Bury Corporation had a number of Regents in service in the 1930s with unusual two-door bodywork. The undertaking's Crossley Condors were similarly equipped.

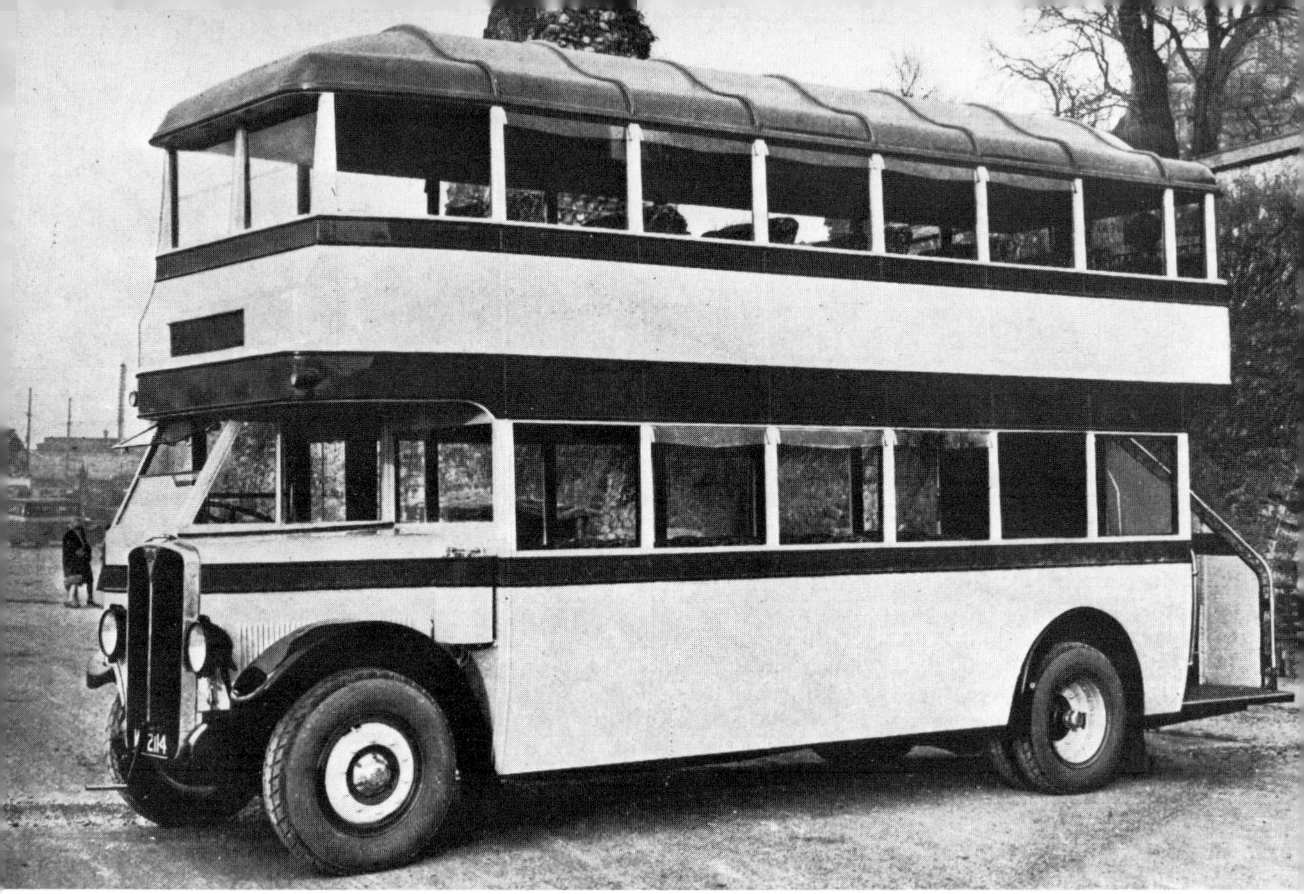

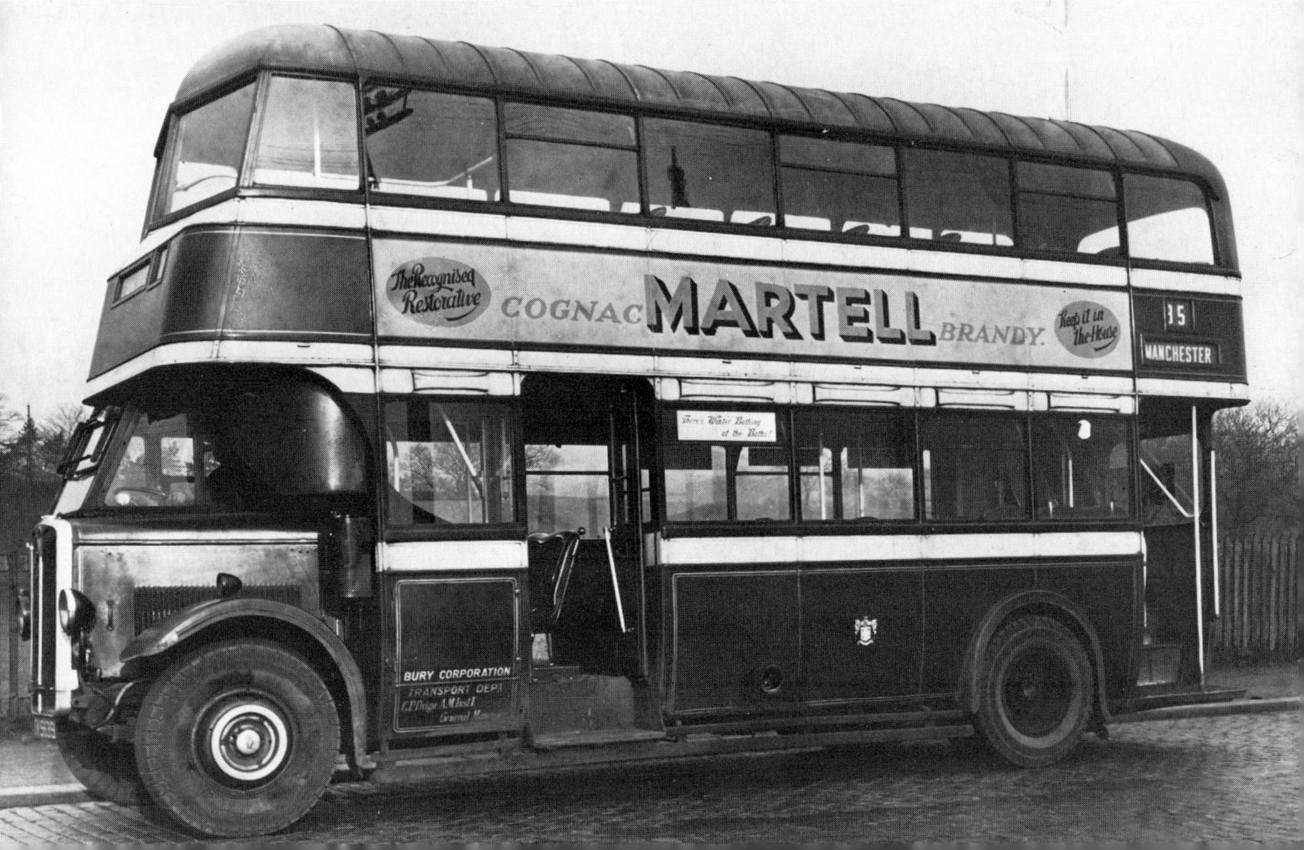
The Recognised Restorative
COGNAC MARTELL BRANDY.
Keep it in the House
35
MANCHESTER
There's Winter Bathing at the Baths!
BURY CORPORATION
TRANSPORT DEPT

MOSELEY AND ACOCKS GREEN 1A
93
AEC
AHX 63
PATTISONS

164A
MAPLES CARPETS Are Best
ST HELIER Av. ANGEL HILL
HIGH ST. SUTTON
BANSTEAD Rd. SUTTON LANE
HIGH ST. BANSTEAD
BOLTERS LANE BRIGHTON Rd.
BLACK & WHITE It's the Scotch!
MORDEN Stn.
ROUTE 164 A
LONDON TRANSPORT
USED TICKETS
BISTO MAKES THE GRAVY
EYK 396

Above left: Photographs of 'Q' buses in action are very rare. This unusual view depicts AHX 63 then owned by the manufacturer running on service in Birmingham. The fact that it was built to a width of 7ft 6in, the then permitted maximum, shows up sharply when one looks at the size of the front windows.

Left: A London RT of the prewar series.

Above: The first provincial example No723 was the intended exhibit for the 1939 Commercial Motor Show that was never held. Here it is ready to enter service in Glasgow complete with a wartime o/s headlamp mask. The nearside would require similar treatment.

provided, and RT1 as it then became formed the basis of an order for another 150 machines to the same specification.

Production had scarcely begun when the Polish excursion of one Adolph put an end to the building of any further sophisticated buses for the greater part of the next decade but the order was completed RT2 — 151 going into service by the end of June 1940. Adolph also put an end to the 1939 Commercial Show for this event that Glasgow No723 was primarily intended.

As it was chassis number 06616963 and the 56-seat rear-entrance Weymann body it carried had roughly a month after completion to contemplate what a centre of attraction they might have been at Earls Court before they began to carry Glaswegians in quantity and that task did not end until 30 September 1955. No723, then looking just a little worse for wear after covering some 500,000 miles, was demoted to driver training and continued as a school bus until the 19 March 1956 when sale to a Manchester dealer took place.

Now it will be appreciated from all this that it was the sole example of the type to be found outside London for almost seven years, but by 1946 Southall was back in business and at this stage a certain undertaking figured in the news when on 1 December 1946, or so my familiar trade journal said, an official handing over ceremony took place.

I have the photograph of the event before me as I write, a wholeplate shot of about a dozen dignitaries who on this occasion at least were not in the centre of the picture. That important space was nicely filled with the shapely form of an LT type Regent which, with about 70 other sisters, managed to escape beyond that frontier which is reputed to exist somewhere just north of Potters Bar, and it made the rest of the fleet obsolescent at a stroke. Nobody ever wanted an 8.8 again and in fact it only needed a garage foremen to book out one of the new Regent IIIs to the same driver on two successive mornings to cause earth-shattering

Above: A postwar Regent III of Cardiff Corporation with the higher bonnet line, screw-fixing sidepanel, and chromium plated radiator shell. A nicely balanced bus.

Left: 'Regent power'. The 9.6litre engine 'in situ' with rocker box covers removed to show the valve springs and tappets. The flexible fuel pipes mentioned in the text run to and from the manifold mounted filter.

dissension in the ranks, so let us consider the specification that was responsible for this near cause of revolution.

Basically everything was new with an engine which clearly displayed its ancestry but was way ahead of its predecessors. The six cylinders had a bore of 120mm and a stroke of 142mm giving a capacity of 9.6 litres. The compression ratio was 16:1 and output 125bhp at 1,800rpm, with a maximum torque of 430lb ft at 1,000rpm.

This was an important feature in a vehicle intended for local stage services where a good rate of acceleration is more useful than high maximum speed, but at the same time the engine was very much quieter than the now-discarded 8.8 litre engine or the companion 7.7 that remained in production. Their merits of good accessibility were however retained, and in addition gear trains replaced the old timing chains and adjusters.

The power output passed through a large diameter fluid flywheel and thence into the frame-mounted gearbox of the Wilson pattern but AEC manufacture, and now for the first time compressed air was used to operate the engaging mechanism so that the old hazards of preselector knee or pedal kick-back injury, and how that could hurt, were gone forever. Final drive was through an underslung worm and wheel mounted at 8in centres and these components had been suitably strengthened to take the power output as had the transmission line which possessed joints of either AEC or Hardy Spicer manufacture.

The gearbox input propellor shaft had a pulley just in front of that component with three grooves to house the triple belts which drove the 9cu ft/min compressor also mounted on the gearbox, and because the latter was set low down and well away from the engine it never was subject to overheating problems. The brakes it supplied had also been much improved over prewar standards, as the linings contained within 16in diameter drums had widths of 3in at the front and 6in at the rear and thanks to the air assistance no great pedal effort was required to ensure a normal stop, although it was easy when first handling this type of bus to obtain the feeling that the brakes were never going to work, there being a little delay apparent due to piston inertia; but this was never anything to cause much worry after some few applications. The brake valve, though, included an emergency device for if one pushed hard the full reservoir pressure of 80psi was admitted to the cylinders instead of the usual maximum of 45psi.

The reservoir itself contained three separate chambers and the incoming air was fed through a composite valve and then into one of them, for the first supplied the brake system, the second the gear change, and the third replenished the other two as necessary. Incidentally the valves controlling the output to these systems were remote mounted. Finally, brake adjustment was catered for by the inclusion of worm and pawl RP type adjusters in each set of shoes.

The rest of the chassis was quite conventional apart from the mounting of the fuel lift pump on the side of the gearbox, and springing was via the usual leaf equipment, but here was yet another innovation for no shock absorbers had been fitted, instead the rear axle had a stabiliser. This was a tube of 3½in diameter that was carried behind and parallel to the axle casing and fitted with substantial arms. One arm was secured through an adjustable link to the underside of the road spring but the other had a telescopic link with a piston that allowed some initial movement either up or down. Once this was taken up as the chassis began to twist (as when cornering) the torque was transmitted to the tube which resisted the action so keeping the bus vertical, but in addition the assembly had another function and that was to keep the axle at right angles to the frame.

Most of these components were, of course, out of the sight of the causal observer but no one could miss the cast radiator which was set low down in the frame thus giving the driver good forward and nearside visibility. This was welcome but not so acceptable was the narrowness of the cab which really gave one little or no elbow room. This was not the only point that caused difficulty one the machines went out into service, although it should be added here that every new design has its teething problems and as the field of operation extends, so do new problems arise. It could be therefore that our troubles were unknown both in London and Glasgow.

Our first two involved the handling and the engine, for a most disconcerting roll was apparent under certain road conditions when the front end seemed to be sliding away, so the wisest course to adopt was to keep the speed down and I often wondered if this was why so few scraped panels were ever evident throughout their long lives. The engine overheating problem was much more serious and eventually the flow of the coolant was revised by AEC to bring a feed direct to the rear cylinder head via a large copper pipe carried along the top of the power unit, and this continued to be a feature of subsequent engines, but, by the time this modification was being applied, the braking system was also under scrutiny for these too were overheating badly and as the drums expanded the automatic adjusters followed up, bringing the clearances back to the designed limits. This of course took place during the working day, then, as the bus stood all night in the depot, the drums cooled down, but the adjusters stayed put until at length the shoes and drums were firmly in contact. The first person to discover the fault would be the early turn driver who would be quite unable to move his bus and then it had to be persuaded on to a pit for rectification. Just to make things more interesting the liners ran off at an alarming and most expensive rate, but it was not long before the fault registered and some redesign work was put in hand.

Some of the remedies applied were incorporated in the first postwar provincial models that came out (in our case from the end of 1947) and they had one easily recognisable feature as the radiator was now higher and had a chrome plated shell. The bonnet layout too was different, with a hinged upper portion and a single side plate that was kept in place by two knurled headed handscrews being easily removable for servicing and yet not prone to rattle as long as they were properly fitted and secured.

The high bonnet provided space for an oil bath air cleaner and whilst it did no doubt improve the rate of cylinder bore wear it destroyed a most useful feature in the process. Incidentally, there was an odd thing here for the makers actually had instruction books ready for issue with the chassis, and that does not always occur — believe me. Now in the London type manual was a frontpiece depicting not an RT but my old Glasgow acquaintance. In the provincial book there was yet another frontpiece, but not this time 723, for a picture of a prewar machine belonging to the same city had been cleverly faked to include the new bonnet

Above: The last Regent III of Ipswich Corporation (No 24) was also the last of its breed.

assembly, something it certainly never possessed, thus presenting a rather fascinating hybrid outline.

The new set up provided a much larger cab area and underneath the structure, attached to the front axle, was another stabiliser so the old rolling symptoms had now been eliminated, with such success that they continued on the single-deck Regal version that was virtually identical to its double-deck counterpart but had a wheel base of 18ft 7in whereas the Regent had axles at 16ft 4in centres.

Another big change from the RT was to be found in the details of the air system for now all the valves were mounted on the tank so that the whole unit could be changed en block at the usual servicing intervals and then quite easily tested on a suitable rig. The braking too underwent other changes. Off came the automatic adjusters and on went a most efficient hand-worked scissors arrangement plus a handbrake adjuster that could be reached from underneath the front of the bus, so there was no need to put it on a pit to do this task until some major re-setting was called for. Lining sizes also changed; widths went up to 3⅝in and 6½in respectively but diameters came down to 15½in thus allowing a thicker drum to be used.

From this time on the Regent became a most reliable vehicle, apart that was from fluid flywheel sealing, for these items leaked oil in no time at all. For quite a period the fault had to be tolerated for there was no alternative to the packing gland, but then twin twin lip seals improved the situation and finally the now ubiquitous bellows gland entirely eliminated the fault. The difference can be summed up by saying that 15 years ago flywheels had to be examined every seven days and would frequently need two pints of oil. Once this amount was lost slip would occur and the wheel overheat so the fault became apparent without there being any need to go looking for it. Now they often go on for a year or more and never need a drop.

Another, but more minor, annoyance came from the fuel system piping. The engines were resiliently mounted and the mountings allowed a lot of rock. The vibration set up led to the unions becoming slack. Then the engine would be covered in diesel oil from the resulting leaks and the heat would set up fuming — a very common reason for changeovers. One pipe which was a particular offender ran to a filter mounted on the manifold. The pipe was long, coming from the injector gallery, and the filter top into which it and a small bleed valve were screwed was of aluminium. Repeated tightening of the pipe which was continually coming loose eventually resulted in a stripped thread and then the top had to be changed, until again another modification, this time involving the use of a flexible plastics pipe, put paid to these antics.

The stabilisers too proved to be something of a mixed blessing for as the springs settled so did their movement vary and at last they would turn over, this state of affairs, if not found on inspection, usually being announced by a rattling noise from underneath. It was not hard to rectify the fault but we always felt that, although the ride was quite good by contemporary standards, they had a bad effect upon springs. This may have been due solely to local factors but it is a fact that 100 Regents between them consumed no less than 443 springs in 12 months time perhaps because their freedom of movement was restricted to an undesirable degree.

I have, though, some fond memories of the Regent III for alas all ours have now departed on the journey of no return, perhaps because the first machine I ever drove in passenger service was of that type, or perhaps because they eased my task as a fleet engineer to a degree that no other bus at that time could have done, not of course that they were free of vice even when the major faults enumerated herein had been eradicated.

In transport anything can happen. For example one afternoon at around three o'clock about 15 Regents stood parked in a neat line at right angles to the garage door and just about in line with the main door pillar. It was bitterly cold and so the doors had been almost closed — almost because men were continually coming in or going out, and through the narrow gap blew a blast that would have made an iceberg shiver. About quarter past three the first teatime peak driver climbed into his cab, started up, engaged gear when the air pressure had risen to the desired level, and moved off through a 90deg turn, then he applied the brakes only to discover that there was a major air leak on the fronts that rendered the bus a complete casualty. The foreman said, 'Take the next', but that was just the same and so were nearly all the others but, despite the panic that ensued, it did not take long to find the cause.

The front brake cylinders were carried on top of the king pins and the push rods to the scissors lever ran through a drilling down the centre of the pin. It was a neat arrangement but the cylinder was in a rather exposed position and in our cases the rubber piston seals had frozen hard and so, losing their flexibility, would not retain the pressure. Funnily enough there must have been at least 80 similar vehicles in use at the time this event took place but although one would have expected them to display similar troubles, particularly if they were running into the wind, not more than about two did so and thereafter we made sure that those doors were firmly closed and personnel used the wicket gate when climatic conditions necessitated this action.

The other thing I always associate with the Regent is the clonk as the driver engaged first or second gear before starting from rest. This noise came from the piston which worked the gearbox bus bar and with it came a jerk which passed right through through the transmission and came out in the body, a jerk which if the bands within the gearbox were not properly adjusted could be surprisingly fierce. Here again though a remedy was available that was quite easy to apply.

The Mark III was a beauty, it would do an enormous amount of work with little attention but if anything did go wrong then rectification could be undertaken without too much trouble. Two men could, for example, change an engine in a day whilst both gaskets could be dealt with by a single man within the same time. Accessibility was surprisingly easy, on one memorable occasion we went out to a defective Regent and found that a push rod had bent so rendering an exhaust valve inoperative. The rod was slipped out, stuck into a gap between two stones of a road side wall, pulled back to something approaching true, re-inserted, and off went the bus once more.

From a driving point of view they were pleasant to handle having a good performance and taut feeling, whilst thanks to the sensibly placed hand brake and air assisted auxiliaries little physical work was involved. Additionally the change speed lever was contained in a gate carried horizontally below the steering wheel so that changes could be made without the need to take one's eyes off the road, and even if a vibration did become noticeable, particularly if the column top rubbers wore, the steering was normally easy to operate.

The Regent III was not a cheap bus to buy and in 1950 an 8ft wide fluid drive chassis was costing around £1,910 but it continued to remain popular almost until the middle of the 1950s when the engine had come to be regarded, due to its thick bearings and separate crankcase and cylinder block castings, as a trifle outdated; production came to an end with the completion in March 1956 of chassis number 9613E 8261, the last of an order for Ispwich Corporation, and after that came the Regent V although that model was first put on public view at the 1954 Earls Court Show.

Maintenance staffs are always agog to ascertain what will replace various well-loved models when their time finally runs out, and usually vent their feelings in precise terms when they are told, or learn, what the management has in store for them, but when the men in a certain place heard, around 1957, that an order had been placed for some AEC Regent Vs which were

to substitute for a like number of IIIs satisfaction was expressed and the new intake happily received.

These buses had many differences from their predecessors. Noticeable at the front was the 'new look' enclosed bonnet assembly beneath which lay the AV 590 engine (or in a few cases elsewhere a Gardner 6LW). The engine was coupled now to a four-speed synchromesh gearbox via a single plate clutch which was hydraulically operated. Another change lay in the air brake system that no longer incorporated a single chamber assembly, but the biggest change of all was apparent in the 30ft long body which had the then new front door position, and this was the surprising cause of the first spot of chassis trouble.

The vehicles had not been in service for a week when passenger complaints about their riding

Left: 'Gardner power'. Only a few Regent Vs were fitted with Gardner engines — one of the Rochdale examples No271 in the attractive livery used by the undertaking in earlier years.

characteristics began to come in. The ride was to say the least 'hard' and particularly so if one was sat at the rear of the bus. The change in door position had had a most unexpected weight transference effect here, and AEC was not the only manufacturer to be similarly caught out. The cure necessitated a revised rear spring which had reverse camber on the two bottom most leaves, and once these had been fitted the complaints disappeared, only by that time the drivers were making some representations.

Their grumble was about a most annoying and yet trivial fault. The accelerator pedal was of the organ type coupled to the fuel pump via a whole, series of pins, and rods. When the joints in the linkage wore the pedal would begin to 'float' everytime the driver removed his foot and so the descent of any hill took place to the accompanyment of a continuous rattle that could be quite disconcerting. No real solution apart from continual maintenance has ever been discovered, for the retaining springs originally tried soon failed from fatigue.

Another characteristic noise was that which came from the gearbox, in fact the whine when lower gear was engaged took one right back to the vintage era, whilst some men never did like the gearbox itself. The actual task of changing a gear was quite easy, and the synchromesh mechanism certainly did its stuff, but the movement required at the gear lever end was very small indeed, and this could in fact leave one wondering whether you actually had picked up for example either second or top.

Another piece of vice was to be found in the clutch-operating mechanism. The clutch was quite easy to operate, but as I have remarked it was hydraulically moved and the big snag did not emanate from the position of the supply reservoir even if this was so situated that over-exuberant filling by the garage staff could result in a driver's shoes being covered in fluid. This particular complaint was unusual, as when the clutch lining wore down there was sufficient play to enable the clutch fingers to move back as a result of centrifugal action occuring when one revved up prior to changing down and until the speed of the assembly was reduced again, the clutch would not grip.

The engines on the whole performed quite well after a little crankshaft trouble in the early days had disappeared for no apparent reason, and, like most AEC power units, had the advantage of exposed injectors. In some designs these components are located under the valve covers so that the upper ends of all the connecting pipes are out of sight. If a union begins to leak, or a pipe fails as a result of vibration, neat fuel can find its way into the sump and the resulting dilution of the lubricating oil then results in some very expensive failures. Full marks to AEC for avoiding that one.

All this series of engines irrespective of size had wet liners, which pushed into the unit construction cylinder blocks and were sealed at the base via two rubber rings one at the top the other at the bottom. The rings gave little or no trouble but in the early days one found that a pin hole would form in the liner, and the gases under combustion pressure then be forced through into the coolant leading a fitter into assuming, not unnaturally, that a gasket had failed, with the net result that several quite innocent gaskets could well be changed before the true culprit was located. A change in liner material and finish was eventually to eliminate all such occurrences.

The engines really had but two problems, and the most noticeable of these to the outside observer was the degree of vibration set up through the engine mountings. This was bad for the passenger, bad for the body, and bad for the mountings as well, as the engine was carried on a mounting ring which lay inside a banjo secured to the frameside members. This banjo had a tendency to crack and when this occurred the engine and gearbox had to be removed and the defective pressing replaced by a new one which was a rather tiresome chore, as pressings came from Southall in an undrilled condition which meant a deal of careful positioning and marking out, in very restricted situations.

Taking out an engine, thanks to the frontal assembly, also caused some difficulty. The service manual included some drawings which indicated a three-stage process calling firstly for the engine to be lifted from its mountngs and drawn forwards until the crane hook came up to the radiator cowl. Here the unit was to be put on to packings so that the hook could be disconnected and brought over the cowl, when the third and last stage would follow with the hook being recoupled to the engine lifting eye, and the engine then whisked away for attention.

We did not like to contemplate having a ton or so of expensive machinery poised in space on the rather dubious bits of wood to be found in the average garage, so a square of about 5in side dimension was cut out of the centre of the cowl, this allowed the arm of the works fork lift truck to penetrate into the under bonnet space where it could be secured directly to the lifting eye and that was the end of that nonsense. The resulting surgery incidentally did not improve the look of the front end as the square was fitted with flanges prior to being finally restored to its old situation. So, when it was back in situ, two lines of rivets showed what had happened but it certainly improved progress.

The AV 590 could progress very well but there can be no doubt that the fuel consumption was rather higher than it might have been and in the end it was this factor plus the relatively small number of buses involved that led to the demise of our specimens, although not before two variants had come into stock. The first of these were later versions of the 590 model and could be distinguished from their earlier counterparts by the rounded front lower edges of the front wings, but there was a further difference under the bonnet, for the engines had distributor type fuel pumps. For some reason these had quite a different note when running, but as this persisted even when certain engine changes gave them earlier type power units, its presence must have been due to other reasons.

They did of course possess all the latest improvements plus the 'new look' front and this truly was an expensive lump of metalwork to keep in good shape. Minor bumps took too much time to rectify, and the wings suffered from galloping corrosion in winter, thanks to the generous dosage of salt dropped on the road by sundry highway authorities. The chromiumed grille sides too were held together in a somewhat nebulous fashion and odd lengths would drop off from time to time to give the vehicles concerned a rather disreputable air. All this applied also to batch number three but here was one of the unsolved mysteries of life.

As the management liked, indeed favoured, the 590 Regent but did not like the resultant fuel bill the decision was taken to purchase a batch with the AEC AV 470 engine, and at once the works prophets began to preach the approach of doom.

Unlike some prophets, though, they were not trying to plumb unknown depths for they already had experience of that same engine in its horizontal form as it was currently employed in sundry Reliance single-deckers. Now these were delightful buses to

Below: Another alternative. This shapely Willowbrook-bodied Regent V of City of Oxford Motor Services (No953) was a vertical 470 engine powered example.

handle but they suffered, despite their rather light weight, from a surfeit of gasket troubles as will be demonstrated in Chapter 8, and it seemed obvious from this that asking the same basic unit to push a vehicle along which had 18 extra seats and another 1½ tons of unladened weight was just asking for trouble, but the prophets were confounded.

An immediate saving of around 2mpg was obtained, most of the gaskets that did fail . . . and they were few . . . would have survived if only some driver had remembered to add a drop of water, and, miracle of miracles, scarcely ever was one changed over for that hardy annual 'pulling poor'.

Now this was all the more surprising as despite what 'they' might have thought the driving staff had never really taken to Regent Vs as a race and those in the engineering department whose job it was to think occasionally about such sad prejudices came up, no doubt quite wrongly, with four reasons, namely — vibration, general unfamiliarity due to the relatively small number, poor nearside vision thanks to the overlarge bonnet, and finally the thin steering wheels fitted.

This final point might surprise the average reader, more than one bus has been changed from sinner to saint simply by having a wheel with a thick rim popped on to the end of the column, but of course the all important question here is . . . Are supplies available?

There are though all sorts of availability. One garage superintendent who was a student of philosophy became tired of having too many Regent road calls, for these had to be inscribed on the changeover sheets and there they attracted the attention of chief engineers and even shinier brass who ought to have had sufficient work (or so he thought) to engage their energies and inquiries elsewhere. Our superintendent was lucky though as the main road which was used by about 90 per cent of his allocation obligingly ran right past the main garage door and so into that door space went a spare Regent all nicely waiting with blank blinds.

The message thus proclaimed that 'A Regent in means a Regent out' was received and understood by all concerned and much less book entry work promptly ensued. The stratagem would not be required now for the Regent double-decker is fast disappearing and many enthusiasts find this a matter of regret.

In June 1965 AEC published details of all chassis built between 1909 and 1964. According to the statistics then presented, 4,102 RT types had been produced from 1946 to March, 1953, in addition to 4,203 of the 9612/3 model. 1,595 of the 9621 version and 132 of model number 6811/2.

The Regent III was thus highly successful and even the Regent V had 2,825 sales to its credit by the December of 1964, but orders were then tending to fall due to the counter attractions of the Routemaster (2,219) the Bridgemaster (181), the Renown, a vehicle which was introduced in 1962, and, alas, the rear-engined buses being produced by other competitors.

The Renown had been specifically designed to allow a notoriously conservative industry to have a lowheight vehicle which gave reasonable saloon headroom and a free choice of bodybuilder. Its introduction followed a period of intense market research to find out just what operators wanted, but the manufacturer was sadly misled when conservatism was for once thrown to the winds and the rear-engined vehicle wholeheartedly adopted. AEC did of course produce one such vehicle, the famous FRM1 which according to rumour had done very well, but this has never been multiplied although some of my friends hoped for years that it would be.

The last medium-weight Regent V chassis number 2MD3RA 645 was completed on 13 February 1968, fitted with the AV 470 type engine, four-speed synchromesh gearbox, and sold to Garelochhead Coach Services, and here is an interesting point, for although the modernised version of this same power unit, the AV 505 (which marked a return to conventional cylinder blocks and dry liners), was

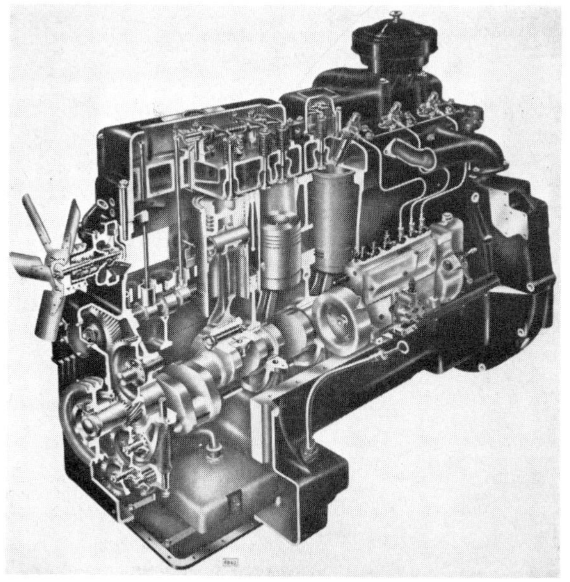

Left: This cutaway view of an H590 engine was included in the AEC service manual and shows clearly the wet liner form of construction employed, the positioning of the sealing rings, and the externally run injector piping, which can never give rise to excessive lubricating oil dilution.

introduced in 1966 it was restricted to truck applications and never installed in a double-deck chassis.

Some such buses, though, did have an engine that, had our superintendents been so equipped, would have rendered the placing of that spare Regent in the doorway quite unnecessary, and here I refer to the AV 691 unit, which, as I know from the few hours I once spent driving a truck so blessed, can really motor. Its use in the passenger world was restricted to fluid drive chassis and the 47th such to be built, number 3D2RA. 2024, was the very last Regent of all. It went down the line on 7 March 1968, was destined for the Douglas Isle of Man fleet, and went to work with that municipality as No15 carrying a Willowbrook double-deck body. It was registered as 410 LMN on the 6 April 1968.

My own colleagues never showed any emotion whenever a Mark V left the fleet, but on the day that the last surviving Regent III passed out of the depot one character who is not noted for displaying his heart on his sleeve muttered in what were suspiciously like tearful tones 'There goes the best bus we shall ever see'.

I was reminded of this profound statement much more recently when I boarded a London RT in the Strand. It was far from new but still purred along as the driver edged his way into Aldwych and Kingsway through a veritable sea of traffic and I had to admit to myself that no other pre-1939 design of bus could be doing such a job of work so well no less than 39 years after its inception. I began to wish I could turn our fleet clock back about 25 years but progress must be made and with that very same process came the next subject for examination, a subject which also has some Southall strong connections.

Below: The last of the line. Regent Mk V No15 of Douglas Corporation is based on the final AEC front-engined double-decked chassis to be built.

8 Some Single Deck Conceptions

The single-deck vehicle has really only taken three forms during the whole of its long life span which covers the entire history of the motorbus industry, although there was a period in the middle of the 1930s when certain experimental arrangements were produced, so although the prime purpose of this chapter is to comment upon heavy or medium weight versions of the latest manifestation, namely the underfloor-engined variety, it is pertinent to pass some comment as to how the type came to achieve the predominat position it holds today.

Until the middle of the twenties almost every bus — inevitably — had the engine tucked under a long and projecting bonnet with the driver seated behind the dash plate. As a result the gearbox (unless remotely mounted down the frame) lay in close proximity to his seat when the gear lever came right against the left hand, and despite all the years that has passed since this first layout was the basic standard we still describe such a vehicle as having 'normal control'.

By 1926 it was however realised that far too much space within the overall box dimensions was being wasted and so there followed the move towards placing the driver along side the engine when some form of connection between the gear lever and the gear box was necessary, thus we came to have the second or forward control arrangement that was so commonplace up to the early 1950s, and which still featured the vertical engine. Even this was somewhat extravagant in space terms and particularly so after the passing of the Road Traffic Act with its attendant length and width regulations which were stringently applied by the certifying officers to give those gentlemen their original title.

The average prewar single-decker thus had a maximum of around 32 seats but traffic was on the increase throughout the thirties and so it was only natural that the more active minds should begin to investigate how the situation might be alleviated.

Alleviation was certainly necessary for I remember only too well the 1930s excursions we used to make once each week to the local cinema three miles down the valley. The programme would end about 10 o'clock thus giving a sufficient interval of time to cross the road and catch the bus which left the market place seven minutes after the hour, but there was always the distinct possibility that we might not obtain accommodation and we were faced with the difficult choice of electing either to see just how Douglas Fairbanks (or one of his contemporaries) dealt with the villains, or walking home. On wet nights the bus always won, for our route was served by two municipalities and a company which employed a good deal of local labour. No village man would have dreamed of leaving his neighbours, for the inhabitants of rural communities in that era knew each other too well for any such anti-social behaviour to occur, but unfortunately the seven minutes past ten was homeward bound to the next town, and the big city boys had a different attitude which can be summed up by the cryptic comment 'thirty-two seats, eight standing, and four bells'.

It was, of course, possible to have bigger buses by employing three axles for an overall length of 30ft was then permitted, and we did for a time 'enjoy' the capacity offered by a variety of Guys and Karriers so equipped, but their reliability was not of the highest order and they started to disappear from the scene at about the time when the side engine position began to be adopted in certain quarters and here we come to the experimental era.

The adoption occurred both at manufacturing and undertaking levels and in the latter case the Northern General company was the main exponent. This concern had some very heavily-trafficked services which contained an unusual quota of low bridges, but there was another hazard at Jarrow where clearances under the Tyneside coaling staithes were very restricted, and it was to overcome the resulting problems that the first SE6 45-seat single-decker was designed.

It was 30ft long, had a petrol-fuelled side valve engine of American origin, a gearbox that came from the same continent, and a single doorway positioned behind the front axle. The following production versions had the same basic components but now the door was brought to the front of the front axle thus giving the vehicle a much more modern look. Little has ever been published about the running of these notable buses but I have an old colleague who worked on them for a time and he tells me that they had three features which caused him to become involved in some interesting development work.

The radiator was at the front and connected to the power unit by some tortuous pipe runs. The engines being well enclosed tended to overheat and this propensity was not helped by the formation of air locks in the aforementioned bends and twists, but the finding of a more suitable layout was an almost impossible task due to the basic layout of the design. Another engine fault was that of high cylinder bore wear caused by the ingress of dust and dirt via the induction manifold. This again was almost inevitable but in this case it was possible to fit a revised air intake scheme by taking clean air from roof level and so long chimney-like induction pipes were fitted.

Trouble number three concerned the actual handling of the buses, and initially a friction dampening device was fitted to the front axle as no shock absorbers had been included in the original specification, but this modification made little or no

Below: Prototype Northern General SE6.

Bottom: A 1933 production SE4.

difference to the major problems which were manifest in wet or icy weather.

The first side-engined buses had three axles, but in an endeavour to simplify the mechanics one of the two rear units was 'dead'. This meant that the front driving axle only needed one differential but the suspension arrangements involved the use of two leaf springs and an inter-connecting balance beam on each side. As a result only about half of the total rear end weight was available for adhesion purposes and so whenever road surface friction was reduced extra care had to be taken when starting or stopping.

The Northern General company must have found the buses to be of advantage, however, as production was continued until 1939 by which time two-axled machines had also been built as had a number of very smart versions intended for coaching duties.

All the later chassis were produced at Southall where the AEC Company had been marketing its 'Q' series of vehicles from about 1933. These also had side engines, and again oil engines were offered in later years as an alternative to the original petrol units, but AEC went rather further than the NGT in including a double-decker in the range. The only substantial customer was the London Passenger Transport Board which eventually had a fleet of around 200 almost all single-deck, but although quite a number of operators bought a few examples it would seem that they were loathe to launch into large-scale purchases due to the relatively high price of the chassis and the overheating/handling snags which were similar to those of the SEs discussed above.

These machines had full fronted body work of a surprisingly modern appearance but by the same surprising coincidence you could have this type of coachwork and still avoid the overheating problems by purchasing yet another advanced model. This was the Maudslay SF chassis which first appeared in the late summer of 1934 at a time when the manufacturers were in a very difficult financial situation. As the designation implies, this was one of the first if not the first, single-decker that could accommodate 40 passengers all facing forwards within the then legal box dimensions (for two-axle single-deckers) of 27ft 6in × 7ft 6in. Some clever design was involved here through the use of a straight and rather high mounted frame which carried the Maudslay made petrol engine of about 5½ litres as far forwards as possible. The front axle was then set back to allow space for a front door and as a result the wheel base was brought down to 15ft so that a high degree of manoeuvrability was available.

It would be interesting to know whether drivers of the time found these vehicles difficult to drive because in the writer's experience the arrival of rear engine buses in the late 1950s or early 1960s caused problems as drivers did not at first realise that as they were sitting well forward of the front wheels they had, in fact, to go beyond a corner before they began to turn into it.

Unfortunately, from the Maudslay point of view, not too many men could have been affected in this way for although the SF40 which was later to be renamed the 'Magna' and acquired a Gardner 5-cylinder engine as an alternative in the process, remained in production until 1939 it would not seem that more than 100 were made but at least it did better than the first true underfloor engined bus which was put on show at the 1937 Commercial Vehicle Exhibition. This was, of course, our old friend the Tilling Stevens Successor which was dealt with in some detail in chapter II because sales figures here never even reached the grand total of one. With the Successor came a somewhat similar goods chassis called the Yeoman simplified to the extent of having only two axles and leaf springs but, again, no one was sufficiently brave to place an order. This sad fact did not deter Tilling Stevens Ltd from building a total of four experimental chassis and continuing with development until well after World War II when according to one of my informants who was so engaged, parts for the horizontally opposed engines were being fabricated from plate. This all goes to prove that the operating side of the motor industry is exceedingly conservative and it is not wise as a result for manufacturers to put too many new innovations into new vehicles. Witness for example the fate of the Guy Wulfrunian of Wolverhampton of recent memory.

Nevertheless, it is interesting to speculate what we might have seen at the Shows for 1939 and 1941 if only they had been held, for by 1939 three other underfloor alternatives had been built. Leyland Motors had a big twin-steer passenger chassis in its new catalogue called the Gnu which possess a vertical engine but just prior to the war starting a somewhat similar but horizontally-powered vehicle called the Panda was produced together with a large batch of what by today's standards would be more conventional machines which again formed a London purchase, the latter though were not so conventional as the single AEC/Park Royal bus that first saw the light of day in the September of 1939. This was surely the progenitor of all presentday front-entrance underfloor-engined buses and not even the lefthand drive or righthand front and centre passenger doors could disguise the fact, for it was intended for the Canadian market.

The home industry had to wait until 1946 and then at the end of the year the firm of Sentinel, of Shrewsbury, began to turn out some unique 7/8 ton goods vehicles which had four-cylinder horizontal oil engines mounted under the chassis frame behind the front axle. It was a short step thence to a passenger vehicle and the first such to be made available in the normal commercial way.

This qualification is most important for the chief engineer of Northern General in SE days was the late Donald Sinclair who later transferred to the Midland Red company. It had a long and successful history of vehicle design and construction already behind it, but Mr Sinclair continued where he had left off when on Tyneside and, after experimenting with rear-engined single-deckers, opted for the underfloor position dropping entirely for postwar construction the vertical-engined single-decker that had been the company's standard prior to 1939. Midland Red thus became the first provincial operator to use underfloor buses in quantity but the arrival of the Sentinel gave others the chance to follow.

The first Sentinel buses were actually a joint effort with Beadle which built the integral 27ft 6in 40-seat bodywork, to a very plain but pleasing design, the substantial aluminium underframe of which carried the Shrewsbury-produced running gear consisting of a 6 litre four-cylinder oil engine, single plate clutch, five-speed constant mesh gearbox, overhead drive worm axle, and leaf springs. Unladen weight was remarkably low at 5 ton 1 cwt and as the engine was rated at 80bhp at 1,900rpm performance ought to have been very reasonable, but before long a larger version was also on offer.

Built to the then newly-permitted 30ft length on two axles only, the 44-seat Sentinel was constructed entirely at Shrewsbury although the previous Beadle influence was very discernible in the clean lines of the body, which now featured an angled driver's windscreen, polished twin bumper bars, and a neat cooling grille of elliptical shape. The extra length put up the unladen weight to 5 ton 15 cwt but the six cylinders provided plenty of urge and a Sentinel of this sort could move along very well.

I remember one of my previous chief engineers coming back from a touring holiday full of praise for the Sentinel coach upon which he had travelled but the type never sold well, and perhaps the reason here was the use of the indirect injection principle in a postwar engine, an engine which sadly came to acquire a rather unfortunate reputation. The pistons projected well above the top of the cylinder block when at the upper end of the stroke and so the heads had to be deeply

Left: Unfortunately the author did not possess a suitable single-deck Q type photograph, but this offside view of a double-decker shows the position of the power unit and the gearbox. The tram type life guard was unusual. The low rear axle adhesion-weight and single rear tyres and lack of front passenger doors gave rise to passenger and handling problems. These could have been solved but the engine overheating propensities and the unorthodox nature of the design were additional factors that led to a commercial failure.

Above: A Maudslay SF40 coach of Red Warrior, then a wellknown Coventry operator, photographed in January 1936.

counterbored to accommodate them. This meant that a large surface area could come into contact with the products of combustion and so a supplement one fully-detergent oil had to be used if ring and piston troubles were to be kept to manageable proportions. Unfortunately, the use of such oils was in its infancy at the time so rather more failures occured than would have been the case a decade later when the adoption was quite widespread.

By 1951 Sentinel had changed to direct injection, and was also producing conventionally-framed passenger chassis but these moves were not sufficient to save the company which sold out a year or two later to Rolls-Royce. That concern turned the Shrewsbury works over to the production of its own oil engines, but it did seem for a time as if further Sentinel type chassis might continue to appear, as a new company Transport Vehicles (Warrington) Ltd was formed for the purpose, acquiring premises in the town contained within the title. A proprietary engine was to have been employed but unfortunately the venture came to nothing.

Sentinel, though, did act as a catalyst if nothing else, for one sizeable operator that favoured the products of an established chassisbuilder wanted some underfloor-engined buses but could not obtain them from the desired source. Recourse to Shrewsbury was thus necessary and in due course orders covering both 40-seat and 44-seat machines were completed and put to work, when it seemed as if a form of physcological warfare was being practised.

Those buses served a certain route which passed a certain works gate, and before long the hint was taken, as I found for myself one night when I turned a corner whilst en route for a game of tennis. There at the stop up the road was a green single-decker of very unfamiliar line, but I was not able to reach it before all the waiting passengers had boarded and the bus rung off. It took me several days to catch up with it when I found that the green paint covered a 44-seat body of Brush manufacture that had what seemed to be an enormously long flat floor, and how strange it was too to hear the noise of the engine coming up from beneath one's feet, although the sound level was quite acceptable. I could not help wondering, though, if it was good engineering practice to sling an engine on its side but one thing here was pretty certain, the chance to answer the question for myself was bound to come along, and come it did although not until three years had elapsed.

The concern I was working for at the time decided

Above: The first of the first production batch of Midland Red underfloor-engined single-deckers.

Above right: Another first production model was this Sentinel-Beadle for H.Boyer & Son, a Leicestershire independent based at Rothley.

in 1952 to buy a batch of new single-deckers that were to replace some prewar 33-seaters that by then were pretty long in the tooth. Obviously underfloor machines were the 'in thing' so it was further decided to split the chassis order three ways to provide three different engines and what it was hoped would be useful comparisons for the future, but this was a minor consideration and what really caused the big thought was just what the bodies should look like.

The drawing office went into a frenzy. We looked at drawings with front, centre or rear doors or a combination of any two and, strange though it may seem now, it was capacity that counted, nobody ever sparing a thought for the possibility that one-man-operation might some day be wanted. Excuses for this apparent omission are not thought necessary for in those palmy days of 25 years ago passengers were still something of an embarrassment quantity wise and every single-decker carried a conductor to cope with the traffic. In the end authority decided to go in for still more comparisons and elected to have front, centre and rear doors, mixing the layouts up amongst the chassis so as to have at least one of everything. The executives of the bodybuilders turned faint when they heard the news for production was not going to be helped by this little package but in due course all were completed.

As it happened no more like them were built and I never became operationally involved as by the time they entered service I had moved elsewhere to find that my new bosses had been in just the same predicament as my old ones. As a result a single order for Royal Tigers, again entrusted to a single bodybuilder, was to have similar body variations, but a few weeks prior to their delivery I had one of my most exciting bus moments on a seat fixed to just such a machine, which was working a long distance cross-Peninne route.

The vehicle had a centre-entrance coach body and the seat by the driver was empty when I boarded, so I made for it and happily watched the world go by until we reached the top of the hills. It had been chilly at 400ft but at over 1,000ft the road was covered with an invisible coating of black ice. This was quite unknown to everyone on board until the driver decided to check his speed which was rapidly rising as we swept down the eastern gradient by applying the footbrake. There was then a 'swoosh', we spun round completely in the road, uprooted a telegraph pole in the process and then began to run backwards down the hill. It was doubly fortunate that nothing was passing and that the vehicle had an open cab for the driver was thrown right off his seat and had it not been for the prompt action of a passenger in grabbing the handbrake we

could well have left the road completely. After that came a second long distance trip when we had another spot of trouble an oil pipe breaking miles from anywhere, and thus I began to have more doubts that were not dispelled when I came to deal with the buses first hand.

As I mentioned earlier we had a nice variety of door positions but all the machines were employed on similar busy urban routes apart from the period when the centre-entrance versions did a stint as crush loaders on a road normally worked by double-deckers, a stint I might add that was not of long duration. As a result about six stops and starts were being made per mile and this had an adverse effect upon the clutches. Matters were not helped by the distance now separating the driver from the engine, for in these early days the former seemed to have difficulty in matching up accelerator position with engine revolutions, and so friction plates began to run off at alarmingly low mileages. This was sad as it meant dropping the gearboxes to make a replacement but very often it was then found that the flywheel insert would be blued or cracked — a sure sign of excessive heat — and so more dismantling had to follow.

The other pieces of friction material in the brakes also wore down at speed although the triple servo system was employed and in our view this was not really man enough for the job it had to do. Consequently much time was spent trying out alternative makes of lining but I cannot recall our achieving very much success.

The engines fitted to these Royal Tigers fortunately did well but they never ran up the fantastic mileages obtained from the vertical 0600 units. We came to the eventual conclusion that a reduction in life of around 25 per cent had to be accepted if you went horizontal and this assessment has been well substantiated over the years all things being equal. Here though we come to the unexpected again, in this instance crankcase ventilation.

The early Royal Tigers had a pipe running from a flange at the top of the sump that was bent through 90 deg and terminated at the upper end at a filter unit which allowed fumes to pass out but prevented road grit from passing in. Unfortunately, there was no baffle inside the sump and so rather more fumes went out than would have otherwise been the case, and this extra loss could have serious repercussions. The Tiger working on that cross-Pennine route would seize from time to time on the last trip of the day when high mileage plus low oil level plus a steep gradient would all combine to produce lubrication starvation, but it didn't take long once the cause was established to find a solution. An extra gallon of oil was added, the dipstick then marked to show the resulting level, and failures became a thing of the past. They still are, even though some quite new Leopards have the same sort of breather for now a revised sump casting whch includes a suitable baffle is produced as standard.

It is of course absolutely essential that any underfloor engine is well sealed against the ingress of grit and dirt and whilst the Leyland scored here the same could not be said about the first Gardner horizontal power units. I had a friend who had a large batch of Guy Arab UFs in his charge and he had all sorts of excessive wear problems in the early days, the fuel pumps being particular sufferers. Gardner soon came to appreciate just what it was up against and the problem is no longer material even though we had some Patricroft engines carried behind the rear axle, a worse position from a splash point of view than that of the midframe situation delivered in later years.

I drove the Royal Tigers quite frequently but was never very impressed by the gearchange mechanism which in my view was far too heavy for comfort, and I am sure that this was responsible for some of our clutch troubles even though they reduced somewhat when we had stronger springs fitted to try to cut down on that reprehensible practice of slipping the clutch whilst cornering, when a lower ratio should have been engaged. But if the Royal Tiger was bad the early Leopard was much much worse, as I discovered on one memorable occasion.

I was on my way home from London by train but instead of staying in my corner seat for the full distance I alighted about halfway and walked the mile or so to the works of a bodybuilder who had promised to have a new Leopard ready for collection that very afternoon. On arrival at the gates I was heartened, having met unkept statements of that nature before, to find it standing ready in the yard so after a quick inspection, checking the oil and water levels, and signing the usual receipt I adjusted the driver's seat, started up the engine and left with the intention of reaching home before dark. I went through the works gates in second turned right and tried to engage third but the lever seemed to be locked solid. After a struggle I obtained the ratio but could not stay in it for long as it was market day in that particular town and traffic was very heavy. Eventually I reached the country but the road home on that pre-motorway day was full of slow-moving trunking vehicles and so a good deal of gear changing was called for.

Within four miles I was suffering from clutch pedal knee, whilst the gear lever continued to be so hard to move that the box felt as if it had been filled with treacle. I reached home feeling quite wretched. Only once before and never since have I been so glad to see the depot doors. The other occasion followed a 200-mile drive with a Gardner underfloor-engined bus with the hardest accelerator pedal it has ever been my misfortune to encounter.

This gear change problem was eventually solved, but as an interim measure a gearbox having a constant mesh second ratio came to be offered as an alternative to the troublesome all-synchromesh assembly and in due course a limited number of these came into the fleet by way of experiment. They proved to be a real trap for the unwary until a little notice was affixed to the dash pointing out the need to double declutch prior to engaging that particular gear but this always seemed to be a rather defeatist approach.

A later and better Royal Tiger era solution could be obtained if you had £2,500 to spend and didn't want clutch troubles by opting for the export-intended Worldmaster, and my chiefs took it. The design proved to be wellnigh indestructable and I would here give the gearbox a special word of praise, but, as usual, we did have some local hazards and the first to become apparent was the fault of the flying sixpence. Worldmasters were reserved for super heavy duty one-man services and they dashed along these particular routes at a speed which raised the traffic superintendent's hair whilst money spilled into the cash tills and sometimes things beyond.

The gearchange control consisted of an air valve mounted on a pedestal hard by the driver's left hand. It was in a most accessible situation and the top of the neat assembly was sealed by a rubber cover through which passed the miniature lever. Continued working of the latter however would cause the rubber to crack and then split and at this point in time someone would be sure to shoot a coin over the till when it would inevitably land on the rubber and slid through the awaiting aperture. It was possible, if luck was on your side, to extricate it with tweezers and bated breath but if the touch of the operator was not sufficiently delicate then some extensive excavation could become necessary and the only good thing you could say about this was that at least it could be undertaken in the dry, for the next fault was rather different.

The air-operated brakes had a liner thickness initially of ¾in and all would be well until this dimension wore down to the $^5/_{16}$in mark when there could be sufficient lift available at the shoes to allow the cams to jam in the on position if anything approaching a severe application was made. This, alas, was where the local factor was met once more for one terminal was on a steep slope. No driver wanted to leave his bus for a 'cuppa' and find it in an embarrassing position on return — although one actually did — so they they would push the pedal down hard and give the handbrake lever a brisk tug just for good measure. Returning refreshed they would attempt to leave with the usual urgent air only to find that acceleration was a negative quantity, when the services of the nearest garage would be sought. Oft times rocking the bus by starting the engine and then quickly going from reverse to first and back again several times would do the trick, but if this failed some unlucky soul had to crawl underneath and try to lever the shoes back and those occasions always arose when it was either snowing or raining.

The other Worldmaster mechanical oddity was

Above: One of the Leyland Royal Tigers in the fleet of the Great Northern Railway (Ireland).

found at the back where the rear axle had a tendency to come slightly loose, when most times the spring bolts would have seized in the brake carrier brackets. The only real remedy then was to take the weight, knock out the spring pins and then wheel the axle and springs out from under the wheel arch to a place where there was sufficient room to swing a 14lb hammer in comfort. When the bolts were out a machining operation was usually necessary after the top of the carrier bracket had been welded up to replace the metal lost by axle/carrier movement.

The Worldmaster, however, had a snag in management eyes for the fuel consumption was rather on the high side, say 7.00mpg as against the 8.50mpg of the Royal Tiger and as high mpg and low maintenance costs were being sought thoughts turned to other possibilities.

Our fleet then, like many others, contained both Leyland Titans with clutches and Daimler CVGs with fluid flywheels. A check on the records would always show, provided the two had roughly equal unladen weights, that there was little to choose when it came to burning up the gallons. But surely what took place vertically should also apply in the horizontal. What therefore had Coventry to offer?

The answer was the Freeline but not the original version with the 10.6 litre engine of six-league boot performance, a thirst to match, and a continuous flow closed circuit brake system that for a variety of reasons — all nasty — could use nearly as much fluid per mile as the motive power division. After one episode with that type no one cared to repeat the experience. Later Freelines though looked more promising. They had air brakes and Gardner engines and, last but not least, many interchangeable components with the double-deckers such as front and rear axle assemblies so it was decided to invest in a few, but then came an unpleasant surprise. The previous underfloor chassis all had a frame height of some 37in unladen but the corresponding Freeline dimension was 41in and the difference was critical.

The undertaking was making frequent one-man conversions at the time and on every occasion shoals of complaints would come in from the more senior citizens about the difficulties they had in negotiating the entrance steps. We tried as a public relations exercise to see every one who wrote to us and explain how the 10in ground clearance regulation of the

Ministry of Transport plus the thickness of the engine plus the depth of the floor and bearers added up to at least 3ft 6in and even if this could have been reduced the wheel must still have remained a problem. You simply cannot expect to carry bus weights on car size tyres but if you could where would the brakes fit? Ladies of mature years, though, are not normally mechanically minded so I doubt if our explanations were appreciated but at least we were always thanked for the trouble taken and usually pressed into taking a dish of tea before leaving.

Obviously something had to be done about the Freeline before it took the road and with the ready assistance of the Daimler Company it was. Firstly the nearside frame member was cut forwards of the front spring front bracket and a 'U' section fabrication was inserted to solve the entrance step problem only now we had another by the driver's bulkhead. A ramped floor was the obvious answer but the radiator top tank was in the way so down went the radiator. Now the entrance platform could be 8in lower than when we started but as the driver's cab floor was meant to be 8in above the frame taking a child's ticket money was going to demand staff with arms like gorillas so it had to descend by a like amount. It was none too difficult to lop 8in off the steering column but this upset the pedal positions so still more modifications ensued. Eventually all this assembly and the cab floor were suitably revised and the result was a quiet well-behaved chassis whose only real snag was a rather low top speed, and here a five-speed overdrive gear box would have been the absolute answer.

The outstanding featue of the Fleetline to my mind was the engine mounting for it was possible to stand a threepenny piece on its edge whilst the engine was running anywhere along the length of the gangway

Left: Among the last AEC Regal IVs to be built were a batch for the Grey Cars fleet of Devon General. RDV 692 had synchromesh transmission and a Park Royal coach body with styling akin to that of Willowbrook. The chassis type was 98225 and the numbers in the 9821/2/3/4/5/6 ranges were built between 1950 and 1957 plus 752 of the 9831 series.

Below left: Daimler's first underfloor-engined vehicle was the Freeline, a real heavyweight that usually had a 10litre engine. A Gardner alternative was offered and was fitted in this SHMD vehicle (67: PLG967). The Northern Counties 34 seat + 26 standing body was of a type that had a vogue in the early 1950s. The bus was a 1952 Commercial Show exhibit.

floor when the coin would stay upright. Fuel consumption was good but it would have been better if only the vehicle had been a little lighter and here the substantial nature of the chassis sides and bracketry was the responsible factor. This was understandable for the Freeline was another bus intended for the export market, but what was not was the failure of Daimler to produce a medium-weight version with all the above advantages instead of leaving the field clear for its competitors. Here without any doubt it was AEC that hit the jackpot.

That company after the 1939 Canadian effort took little or no interest in the underfloor field until 1949 when the first Regal Mark IV was announced. This was another heavyweight with fluid transmission as standard and powered by a horizontal version of the famous Regent Mark III engine which like the Crossley of old had dry sump lubrication.

The maker had one of the lefthand drive form on its stand at the 1950 Commercial Show and according to the official guide the asking price was £2,233 but one can safely assume that as this was almost 32ft long the shorter home model would be rather cheaper. The synchromesh version certainly was for one of these was also on display (as a Crossley) and in this case the price tag read £2,178. The biggest home customer was London Transport, relatively few being sold elsewhere. In fact the only colleague I knew who had any never grumbled about what they could do, but simply at the fuel used in the doing. We were all fuel cost conscious at that time, so it was no real surprise when a visit to Southall in 1952-53 brought me face to face with the first Reliance chassis, then in an almost completed state.

The Reliance came into the medium weight range and my first association began when a demonstrator arrived and I was able to have a run with it on service. I thought it to be an ideal machine. The steering was light as were all the other controls and I was particularly impressed by the five forward speed all synchromesh gearbox that was easy to use and which like all AEC parallel shaft units required only a small movement of the gear lever knob to vary the ratio.

Not so good was the engine mounting that brought out a good deal of vibration at idling speed into the saloon but the engine, in this case a 470 unit, performed well and returned a fuel consumption in excess of 10mpg during its stay with us. A fortnight, though, is not really sufficient to bring out all the vices and virtues and the engine possessed quie a few of the former, as we found when our first were received into stock.

The engine as mentioned in the Regent V part of Chapter 7 had wet liners with rubber sealing rings and leaks in the horizontal version were not unknown, but far worse were the all-too-frequent gasket failures for Reliances boiled on all sorts of occasions. Putting a new gasket in was never a big job on an AEC power unit, but whenever the water temperature reached a high level the gauge would also give up the ghost. This was of the bulb type with a capillary tube running from the steering column mounted instrument panel through the cab floor and then along the chassis to the bulb housing which was located in the thermostat casting. Numerous clips held it in place so when a failure did occur a good deal of time had to be spent in freeing all the screws or bolts, threading in the new connection, inserting the bulb in the aforementioned housing and then cleating everything up again. The thermostats too were a source of trouble for if one should stick a gasket failure was automatic and here was another awkward job. The housing was located in the main engine water line behind the radiator and very close to the floor on a completed vehicle. Eight bolts held it in situ and, as they were bound to be seized, cutting off would be necessary — a task that the garage staffs did not appreciate.

All this occurred when the vehicles were used on stage carriage duties but was never absent on the coaches despite the lighter work they did and here was a very bad fault. Any vehicle which carries passengers for any length of time needs heaters but one small leak at a gasket would allow air to bleed into the heater piping. An air lock would follow and the whole system thus be rendered inoperative, an event that usually occurred when around 10 miles out from the start of a long distance journey. Then cold passenger feet would result in hot passenger complaints.

Needless to say various attempts were made to find a cure, and one early essay was to move the water pump from the front of the cylinder block to the auxiliary drive box so as to improve the flow, but this only increased the number of water joints in a pipe layout that would have made a water distribution engineer green with envy. Water leaks also formed an ever-present hazard and one concern I knew had a standing instruction that every piece of rubber coupling hose and they were many had to be renewed at a regular interval of time.

Another series of modifications covered the cylinder head studs and here one came to the heart of the matter for with a .004in nip on the liners, gasket failures should just not have happened. There were 13 studs which ran well down into the block and they naturally expanded as things warmed up. Their length was such that expansion could exceed the nip and in extreme cases it was possible to go beneath an idling Reliance as it stood on a pit, look up, and watch the cylinder heads 'dancing' on the block.

All this was a tremendous shame as the Reliance then costing around £2,200 in synchromesh form must otherwise have been an outstanding success, for it certainly made an very good coach or dual-purpose chassis and here its excellent ride and general quietness were of obvious advantage. The rest of the assembly was also very good, rear axle or steering faults being virtually non existent, whilst the brakes, triple servo at first and air pressure later were always well on top of their job.

Eventually around 1966 when about 6,000 chassis had been sold the new 505 engine became available. This was similar in general appearance to the 470, and did in fact employ the same crankshaft forging, but the top end was new for the cylinder block now had pressed-in dry liners and the heads were kept in place by 14 short studs that laid the old expansion bogey firmly to rest. Another innovation was the fitting of a distributor type fuel pump driven off the end of the compressor drive for air brakes now became standard.

If you wanted more Reliance power bigger engines were available, either the horizontal version of the 590 or, when that was withdrawn, the larger 691, but as the 505 could provide the extra power to propel the 32ft long machines being acquired at the time we turned over to the former and as usual with anything new in rolled the problems, and the first was quite unique.

The 505s went into service in batches of one for thus were they received from the bodybuilders, but by the time five should have been at work two were reposing in the works with seized engines and all the evidence pointed to a distinct lack of oil. The night staff responsible for topping up swore great oaths that they had faithfully checked the levels and certainly the sheets had been ticked off against the appropriate fleet numbers but no replenishment had been booked to them. Grave doubts were thus rasied in certain minds as to what was truth and what was fiction and these were only resolved when a highly-thought-of member of the supervisory staff was sent on safari to make a detailed inspection.

He returned promptly to say the levels were satisfactory but one bus seen was actually stood in a depot at the time and a few minutes after he had left the premises it was picked up by the chargehand greaser who had it on his list as wanting an oil change. He ran the vehicle on to the pit, undid the sump plug, and out dripped about three drops!

To say there was consternation was putting it mildly. A high level tribunal went off to ascertain the true facts but there was no oil in that sump and at this stage one member idly pulled out the dipstick to find it showing 'Full'. The cause — wrong dipsticks — they were too long and when pushed down their tubes bent to lie along the base of the sump where they could scrape up sufficient lubricant to cover them to the full mark. Needless to say certain remedial action followed forthwith and no similar failures occurred thereafter.

After this episode it was found that oil consumption was on the high side which obviously hadn't helped in the early days so the rings, and later the rings and pistons, were changed when a substantial improvement was shown, and then came fixing device fault number two.

Because the 505 had dry liners different coring arrangements were neccessary when casting the blocks and this meant that a cover plate had to be provided along the top face. The plate was long and behind it of course on a completed engine was part of the cooling water space. It was held down by a number of set screws, but continual expansion and contraction as the engine became hot or cold could lead to them fracturing and then water would pour out from the resulting hole. Carrying out a repair would have been easy if only the plate had not been located behind the fuel pump and compressor and the net result was thus still more dismantling unlimited.

Once more these initial troubles were ironed out one by one and once more they all related to the engine department. The rest of the chassis was trouble-free and once again the gearboxes deserve a special mention, particularly so in the case of the semi-automatic units. They just went on and on, no doubt because they were working well within their limits when taking the power from the 505 engine and also because they were in a situation where an adequate flow of cooling air was available. This is not always the case as the next chapter will show.

The Reliance is still available being updated only in 1971 when the wheelbase of the interim length version was changed from 16ft 4in to 16ft 2in so that a door whose width would comply with the Bus Grant regulations could be fitted. The Leyland Leopard also

Right: One of 30 MCW-bodied Leyland Royal Tiger Worldmasters delivered to Glasgow Corporation in 1957-58. The interiors were fitted out by the undertaking.

HILLINGTON
15
LS30
FYS 876

comes into this popular category. We came to acquire two later batches of the Leopard both having the 0600 engine and fluid transmission, and on one of these we found that our old flying sixpence form of gear change unit was again incorporated. Both have proved to be very reliable even when allocated on a regular basis to the notoriously severe routes that formerly taxed the Worldmasters, but they have one feature which is not appreciated.

On the Worldmaster (and the Reliance) the engine and gearbox are some distance apart and connected by a carden shaft. This means that the rear of the fluid flywheel is not only open to the atmosphere and hence cooling but also for easy inspection. In the Leopard, however, the aforementioned units are linked by a substantial casting which almost completely surrounds the flywheel. These have suffered very occasional gland failures when the gearbox has to be dropped which is bad, but what is worse is the fact that one cannot tell if the new gland will seat properly until everthing has been put together again.

All the above remarks applied to the earlier generation of underfloor engined machines but by the middle of the 1970s the position had greatly changed. The Daimler Freeline, the Guy Arab and, very surprisingly, the corresponding Bristol model had all disappeared whilst the Reliance seemed to go into a decline once the AEC concern, like the other three manufacturers mentioned above, had become a part of the British Leyland empire. The Leyland Leopard, though, continued to become the best selling chassis of its type and its appeal was certainly strengthened when the 0.680 engine became available, which produced sufficient power to cope with the heaviest stage carriage duties or to propel a heavy coach body along a motorway at speeds in excess of 60mph. By this date, too, transmission fashions had changed and very, very few Leopards were being built with conventional gearboxes, the pneumocyclic version being almost universally employed but a synchromesh box can still be obtained on the Reliance although this is now a proprietary unit instead of being of Southall design and manufacture.

Despite its success, the later Leopards do, though, have one or two 'quaint' features and perhaps the worst of these is the standard of ride given by the 10 or 11-metre chassis. Various spring assemblies have been used at the front including particular units which have a different number of leaves in the off and nearside positions, but you will note the omission of the 12-metre version from this complaint. It, being a later design, benefited from some more recent technology and in this case the springs, instead of having conventional pins and shackles, terminate in a resilient moulded rubber device that gives much improved characteristics. I suppose the Leopard had two other irritations, namely the noise levels emitted by the

Below: This Marshall-bodied AEC Reliance 470 was new to the City of Oxford in December 1962.

engine and by the rear axle, something I always note when I travel in a coach, but they are a nice vehicle to handle particularly since power steering also came to be incorporated into the specification and truly, from a driving point of view, there is no comparison between working on a synchromesh Leopard of, say, 1968, and a semi-automatic version of 1978.

I like to have the odd Leopard drive but the vehicle that really took my breath away was an underfloor engined Volvo. I will have to refrain from making any detailed mention of this machine or of the other currently available underfloor engined model, the Seddon Pennine, at this stage but the Volvo is worth a few words. The first one I ever drove had a synchromesh gearbox and the control system had obviously been designed for the left hand drive position. It was, as a result, very difficult to decide just what gear was where, but specimen number two had a semi-automatic gearbox so no such problem existed. The big problem now was that of keeping down to the speed limit for a combination of five gears plus a turbo-charged engine meant that one swept along the motorway with effortless ease and, in any event, didn't really have to change down more than about once in a hundred miles.

The engine is, of course, the Volvo six-cylindered 9.6litre 2306hp turbocharged unit which has the most admirable feature of having each cylinder bore covered by its own separate cylinder head. Here is a maintenance feature to be admired, but at this stage let me add a note of caution.

As an industry we could not have done without the underfloor engine for it made large scale one-man conversions possible and, of course, by allowing all the box area to be used basically for passengers, it improved the ratio of income to operating costs despite what might be written here; so why the caution?

Well, this book is really all about maintenance and all the time the relevant national or international regulations become ever more stringent. One subject under discussion in legislative circles at the moment concerns the introduction of more onerous noise regulations and we are already seeing the emergence of the 'quiet' double-decker on to the market but that quietness is achieved in the main by shrouding the engine and gearbox, etc. Consequently, the mind boggles at just what sort of job the maintenance of a fully encapsulated, turbo-blown underfloor-engined bus would be. We might then have engineers sighing for the return of the front vertical engine in the same way that many now long for a return to front engined double-deckers but, as chapter IX will show, I doubt if we will be able to escape from those 'troubles behind' in the foreseeable future.

Below: General chassis layout of a later AEC Reliance unit fitted with the 505 engine. Note radiator expansion tank on nearside, fan cowl, dropped chassis extension and large air cleaner.

9 Troubles Behind

About 30 years ago I had to make quite a long journey when travelling to or from work, and the quickest way to complete this was to catch two trains, one main line, one branch, but the latter which was a Great Central period piece in itself only perambulated up and down its six miles of track which comprised roughly half the trip, at infrequent intervals so if I was not able to leave the works precisely at 5.15pm four separate rubber-tyred alternatives were involved, the first of which sprouted a pair of trolleys.

Now I always took rather a jaundiced view of the trolleybus, as it was neither one thing nor the other and, if the 'other' was a tramcar then there was my favourite, but these trolley vehicles had been responsible for the demise of the trams along that very stretch or road just before the war commenced and looking back in retrospect I can see that this fact was one of the main reasons for my prejudice.

The only good thing I could find to say about them was that, as a high proportion had three axles, their carrying capacity was useful but conversely a power cut or electrical failure would affect the lot, and, as such occurrences usually took place in the rush hour, during a winter's evening commuting could become a form of endurance test.

Then I would contemplate what could possibly replace them and still give the same number of seats, and here was a pleasant spare-time occupation. After eliminating several alternatives I came to the conclusion that my ideal would take the form of a Roe composite body mounted upon a Daimler chassis but not the sort of CVG5 that the same municipality favoured when it sent an odd order in a Coventry direction. My fancy, still being tinged with Karrier memories, had been taken instead by a press report of the CVG6/6 three-axled machines Radford works had built for export to Cape Town in 1948. I should add here that I was initially a little apprehensive as to the performance that would be given by the 6LW power unit, but finally came to the conclusion that the power to weight ratio would be no worse than that of the CVG5 so why not have a try? (There were incidentally 20 in the batch with chassis numbers in the range 14235 to 14254 inclusive).

Strangely enough, some while later, I actually joined the engineering department of that very trolleybus operating concern, and one day I mentioned the foregoing to my chief, but that gentleman who had been actively concerned with the design of trolleybuses in his earlier days gave me in very succinct terms some good and sufficient reasons as to why double drive axles should avoided at all costs, and there languished another spark of genius . . . or so I thought; and then I missed the obvious.

An acquaintance invited me almost simultaneously to spend a day viewing the Foden factory, and whilst walking through the Sandbach shops we came across a rear-engined coach chassis that had to become the subject of a detailed inspection. Now I had seen these quite often on the road, as our local coach operators had taken to them in quite a big way, two-stroke engine and all, but I had never seen one employed on stage carriage services so I asked the question as to how many had been produced specifically for such type of work?

If I remember correctly the answer was — 'One' — which was then running in the Potteries and rightly or wrongly I gained the impression that Fodens had never been very concerned to promote rear-engined bus as opposed to coach sales. Perhaps the limiting factor here was the type of transmission employed which of course included the Foden brand of constant mesh gearbox. That could not be regarded as being wholly suitable in any event for stage carriage service and particularly so when it was coupled to the far end of some very remote gear changing linkage.

Some time went by which was filled with a move and various strange and unconfirmed rumours and then one day the telephone in my new office rang and I picked it up to find the excited chief engineer from the

Above: A 1938 design of rear-engined single-decker typified by the preserved CR class FXT 120 contrasts sharply with the conventional T class vehicle of the same period also saved from the scraphead. The frontal appearance of the CR was stylish but wasted a good deal of useful floor area.

company up the road on the other end of the line. Now I have shown previously how the 'Old Pals Act' applies in the transport world, but I must add here that a little professional needling is often involved as well, and so when my caller suggested that I should 'Come and see what I have got' he made no attempt to hide the 'one-upmanship' in his voice. Well I accepted his invitation to meet him in a nearby bus station about an hour later and there all ready to enter service on one of his company's intertown routes and almost hidden by a crowd of curious busmen was the first rear-engined Leyland double-decker to go into revenue earning service the very famous STF90.

This machine as enthusiasts will know had had a fully-fronted Saunders Roe body, with a rear staircase and platform a part of which was taken up by the engine casing, in this case housing a turbocharged version of the 0.350 Leyland vertical engine.

We travelled the eight outward miles as passengers, and then I was invited to pass through the almost unique front bulkhead sliding door and take my place in the driving seat, which I did with some trepidation. Fortunately this vehicle was quite easy to drive as from an axle positioning point of view it scarcely differed from the orthodox Leyland PD2 and the preselector gearbox made ratio changing easy, but one had to be very careful nevertheless as the air brake valve was most finely adjusted, and when I first attempted to pull up at a stop I almost had about seven alighting passengers coming through that bulkhead door after me.

It seemed a bit queer to be driving without being able to hear the engine noise except rather indistinctly, and we both came to the conclusion that here could be a significant snag. We felt similarly too about the platform arrangements, but obviously this was a newcomer that was going to be worth watching, as there was certainly nothing wrong with its performance.

I had one or two other rides on the vehicle in the week that it was in our area, but then things went quiet again although a sight of the sister machine registered XTC 684 in Bolton sometime later made me appreciate that things in Leyland were still moving. This latter bus to my mind had a very attractive front end with its curved dummy bonnet that actually provided space for the batteries and fuel tank, and was a virtual replica of the arrangement fitted to the London Transport TF and CR type vehicles of prewar vintage and in fact the combination of a half-cab, low bonnet line and no engine noise seemed almost too good to be true to one who was still accustomed to 5LW solid mounted orchestrations. As things turned out so it was, because the next machine to appear in the series took on a rather different form and here we had the true progenitor of the Atlantean as we know it today.

I caught my first glimpse of 251 ATC at the

Commerical Show of 1956 and glimpse is perhaps an overstatement as it was certainly the star attraction, and almost hidden under a crowd of admirers or critics, but the latter seemed to be very much in the minority. This vehicle had the now ubiquitous front entrance, staircase, layout and general arrangement plus the 0.600 power unit, but there there were other innovations under the panelling. The body was built on the integral principle, and because of this there were some internal stiffeners that must have made the design a hit with any bus riding courting couple who might have chanced to use it.

The rear axle was of the double reduction form, and at the other end independent front suspension was provided via the medium of a pair of torsion bars, and these certainly gave a very high handling/ride standard, something I can personally vouch for because very early in 1957 I was able to ring my friend up and invite him to 'Come and see what *I've* got' for the bus was left with us for the best part of a week to see what we thought about it, and I was thus able to take it out on several occasions.

As it was not licensed we could only use it on test runs, so it never carried any of our farepaying passengers, much to the disgust of the local enthusiast fraternity for its sensational green appearance gave rise to a great deal of comment. My main impressions were again the silence, the excellence of the road holding qualities, and the different coloured segments on the speedometer which were provided so as to give one some indication of when to change gears, but it was fairly evident that this form of vehicle was going to be an expensive one to produce and would have the disadvantage, moreover, that, as Leyland no longer built psv bodies, it would have either to come back into that business or farm out production to some other concern with a consequent restriction on customer choice.

It was not surprising therefore that when just prior to the 1958 Show the details of the production version were announced, some further major changes had been made. Now the Atlantean had a separate chassis, of 16ft 3in wheelbase, and all the motivating bits assembled into an easily interchangeable power pack that included the engine, centrifugal clutch, four-speed semi-automatic gearbox, radiator, and angled drive units. The latter was another innovation because the double reduction axle had been dropped in the interests of prime cost, and a spiral bevel substituted instead, which necessitated the use of a rather unorthodox diagonally running propeller shaft. This led to a little snag as the centre line of the shaft at the axle end was higher than the centre line of the road wheels, so the floor at the back of the vehicle had to be raised to provide the requisite clearance, and this to some extent destroyed one of the most appealing features of its one-piece predeccessor in that the overall height had to be increased.

This in turn led to the introduction of alternative lowheight or normal bodies, and the former could squeeze under 13ft 4in bridges although the rear upper saloon seats had then to be arranged to give a side gangway a step which reduced the capacity of 78 on the standard model down to 73.

To my mind most of the early Atlantean bodies were something of a disappointment as I never did like single-skinned domes, or slabs of that horrid chequer plate aluminium material, or painted inside panels, nor did I appreciate the high upper saloon waist rails that seemed to be so unnecessary, but I could see that whilst an operator might do something about the former in his specification he was not going to be able to change the latter unless he could persuade the body builder to revise some drawing office opinions. Still these were only really details. The big question for any fleet engineer was 'Does it work?'

I am afraid here that we lagged a bit. Readers may recall that there were four Atlanteans at that show, for Glasgow, Wallasey, Maidstone & District, and James of Ammanford respectively. The Wallasey example fleet number 1 registered FHF 451, must have built up quite a mileage before my first machines took the road, for if chassis numbers are anything to go by then ours were about 400 from commencement.

It is interesting here to recall that we paid £3,040 for the chassis and £2,850 for the bodies although the last figure needs to be qualified for it only covered essentials and so we parted with another £300 or so, to include heaters (at £98) double top rail sets with moquette, stainless steel handrails, more indicators, treadmaster in the gangways and various other mod cons which brought the grand total up to £6,207 18s 9d, and when we had settled up for all the batch we felt we had parted with a king's ransom, only we didn't know what was coming. A batch of rather similar buses ordered for 1978 came out at £35,000 so it's a good job a 50 per cent grant can still be obtained, but to return to 1960.

On the first morning with some trepidation we handed over those first Atlanteans to the traffic staff, and waited for the results which were not long in coming in. They were put to work on a heavy service, and the crews took to them like ducks to water once the drivers had mastered the best way to manipulate their bulk through therather narrow streets in the town centre, and here we had our fair share of bashed panels, but that was only to expected.

Needless to say I dusted off my psv badge and had a go myself, and I came away convinced. People may tell me what a difficult job a city bus driver has in today's traffic conditions, but my basic reply thanks largely to the Atlantean is 'bosh'. I would much rather

Above: The first manufacturer to build rear-engined psv chassis in quantity postwar was Foden. This example which has the manufacturer's own two-stroke supercharged engine was on display at the 1951 Festival of Britain exhibition. A substantial machine that deserved a success it never achieved.

Right: The engine mounting of the first prototype Atlantean behind the rear platform.

spend hours in such a bus, traffic or no, with little noise, lighter steering, and be able to control the loading, than minutes in the cramped cab of the average PD2 with a heavy clutch and gear change, plus a bell ringing in one's ears every second or so. Here I am not disparaging the PD2 for every forward engine half-cab machine must possess the same inherent disadvantages.

But this was on the road, feelings in the garage were more mixed. We had higher fuel consuption, fuel pump troubles, noisy centrifugal clutches, gearbox failures, and a run on brake liners, but taken all in all we could not really grumble although management still could not refrain from trying something else that was new, as soon as it had the chance to do so offered.

I well remember going to Coventry in 1960 and looking in then at a certain bus production line which contained that week's output... just five chassis, but the same day I was shown a drawing that was going to change things somewhat for it revealed the form that the new Fleetline chassis might eventually take.

Daimler imitated but it also tried to improve, and the startling innovation about the Fleetline was the ingenious method of building a gearbox with two concentric shafts, the inside one taking the drive right through the unit to the far end whence it travelled back to the output gearing via the epicyclic trains encountered on route. This with the further assistance of a double-reduction axle, kept all the transmission line on one level, eliminated the need for the higher lower saloon rear floor and hence that for two different types of body.

Still under BSA Group management the company had employed its own 8.6CVD6 engine which was then out of normal production and added a turbocharger to obtain a sufficiently high power output. Here incidentally were the fruits of some development work done about 1955 in which we had been involved when it was found that whereas the maximum power output when naturally aspirated was 108bhp at 1,700rpm the fitting of a turbo-blower could lift this figure to about 118bhp, a most useful improvement.

The first of the line, chassis No60000 and registered in the autumn of 1960, was to become famous as 7000HP and came to us in its blue Birmingham livery. It performed very well and was actually one of only three Fleetlines to have Daimler Mark VIII engines, the other two being No60001 which was utilised by the experimental department and 60.002 the show chassis, both of which were subsequently dismantled without ever carrying a body, whilst 7000 HP itself was later to lose its Daimler power unit for one of Cummins manufacture, something it retained when finally sold to the Willington-based Blue Bus concern of Messrs Tailby and George.

Management, as I have remarked, was intrigued and so we went both ways in the interests of science ordering Atlanteans at £3,023 each, and a few Fleetlines at £3,130 but note here how one price had dropped. Could this have been the result of competition, better manufacturing processes or a combination of both factors?

In the interval, though, before our buses came we had the visit from yet another demonstrator, one of the 14 pre-production chassis that were produced consequent upon the decision to drop the Daimler engine in favour of the Gardner 6LX, but in my view if the company's virtually unbreakable CD650 106 litre engine had been adopted instead of the Mark VIII then Daimler power units might well have been with us for a while longer.

Our plaything, chassis No600015, was the Northern Counties-bodied and magnificently-finished vehicle that was intended for the T. Hunter portion of the A1 fleet. (The others went to Birmingham Nos004 to 013, Sunderland No014, Tailby and George Blue Bus No003, and lastly somewhat out of sequence No027 to Potteries Motor Traction.) This A1 vehicle was noteworthy in having the fairings above the engine compartment that eliminated the somewhat unsightly bustled effect that had been with us since the time of the first Atlanteans. This vehicle made a most profound impression upon all who came into contact with it, because in our view both the suspension and the fuel consumption were better than those of our competing Atlanteans although the latter possessed a livier performance, and this mark you was in the days before the 0.680 engine had been made available.

Our first Fleetlines followed close upon its heels, and these not only had the fairings but also another improvement in their one-piece front windscreens, and here in my view is a piece of development work that is worthy of the highest praise. There is just no comparison in the visibility available from the old two flat glass/thick pillar construction, and that given by these fantastic pieces of curved glass.

Well it is now almost 20 years since I first shook hands metaphorically speaking with my first rear-engined charge and over the years the percentage contained within the fleet has slowly grown, so perhaps it is pertinent to consider how we stand with them at the moment.

In my view buses of this sort are first and foremost a tool of the traffic department, thanks to the high seating capacity and readiness with which they can be converted to one-man operation. It could well be that this is as far as the average fleet engineer would be prepared to go on the credit side for it is becoming increasingly obvious that some authorities are of the opinion that the type is rather too susceptible to failure for their liking, but is this feeling really justified?

All my colleagues at that 1956 Show were concerned with the damage that could occur to the engine and its auxiliaries in the event of another vehicle coming in through the back bonnet lid, but in all the thousands of miles hours have now run nothing of the sort has ever occurred, although they are often to be found in the bodyshop having panelling replaced. Usually this stems from the driver forgetting again that he is at least four feet in front of the front axle and not making sufficient allowance when cornering. If you

Left: The first and second Atlantean prototypes after considerable demonstration work passed into the hands of Lowland. The similarity of the front end treatment of the second machine to that of the prewar CX class single decker will be noted.

Below left: Completed vehicle 281 ATC, as the final product became, was attractively finished in a green livery, the MCW 78-seat body having clean lines externally although the internal stiffness needed gave the lower saloon a rather cluttered look.

look at the content of almost any fleet you will see that a percentage will inevitably show bruising just in front of the rear axle as a result, but we have had some front ends to rebuild as well and impact has not always been responsible.

I rightly praised on an earlier page the big front screen but it is a heavy component and the effect of this weight was not appreciated in the early days. The screen could make the front dash tend to drop when the glass fibre frame would wear and the glass become loose, so now all new bodies have extra stiffening and often a substantial tie rod running vertically from dash to cant rail on the centre line of the bus as well, but another cause of front end problems came from the lack of ground clearance on roads which suddenly experienced a change of gradient. In more than one town a certain amount of highway surface relevelling has been called for, often at rather short notice.

The form of body construction employed has also had a repercussion at a little above ground level for the platform floor being usually of the one-step type has to be made from metal sheeting and this acts as a sound board, reflecting and enhancing any rattle which might come from loose spring clips or worn shackles so that in extreme cases passage over a pothole is marked by a noise that can be of quite alarming proportions. Those big passenger doors too might look very nice and keep most of the draughts out but they also can cause trouble when the linkage wears, or goes out of adjustment, and doors are somewhat expensive things to purchase or repair. If, of course, they should fail in traffic the bus has to be taken out of use and so availability is adversely affected, for no substantial reason.

The enclosing of the platform, though, leads quite automatically to other problems. Seventy or eighty passengers breathing nicely together means that a good deal of water vapour is produced inside the bus and kept there. Add to that the moisture content of a

Above: One of the earlier lowheight Atlanteans of Maidstone & District beside the preserved Hastings trolleybus.

Above right: Rutland Clipper. Another early rear-engined venture was the Rutland Clipper built by Motor Traction Ltd and bodied by Whitson. Fitted with a Meadows engine it appeared in 1954.

wet afternoon say in Manchester, and let the ambient temperature fall somewhat thus keeping the windows closed and then condensation on the windows in general and the front screen in particular becomes such that the outward view is rendered virtually non existent. At this time a good demisting unit is essential but one thing that most rear-engined buses lack is a sufficient supply of hot air at front dash level. This is not surprising as the outlet slots will be around 30ft from the heat source but in addition the working fluid which naturally wishes to rise, having a low density, has to be persuaded to fall as the demister will lie below the level of the top of the cylinder block and heads, and matters will be worsened if the temperature is so low as to allow icing to occur.

In previous years it was possible to take the demisting intake from the lower saloon but the bus grant scheme now calls for the adoption of a fresh air supply as standard so the ingress of chunks of ozone at around, say, minus two means that the already overladen heater has to work that much harder and usually it is incapable of so doing. One alternative is to have electrically heated screens but these are very expensive and give rise to other difficulties.

The bus heating system generally was improved when it became possible to install the heat transfer coils under the upper saloon rear seats so that they are right above the aforementioned heat supply. Air can be taken from the back of the bus while access to the motors or coils is easy once the seat cushions have been lifted. The shut-off valves are readily available and the pipe runs are reduced to a minimum but even so leaks can occur and the poor quality of the average water joint has become a matter of concern to many operators, some of whom are now taking active steps to find a better alternative.

Heat availability does, though, depend to a large extent on engine combustion and it follows from this that if a naturally cool running engine is fitted then the amount of heat passing from the unit into the heater radiators is never going to be over excessive and it would not seem here that the old expedient of blanking off some of the main cooling radiator area is of much value where rear power units are concerned. Nor from our experience do thermostatically-operated radiator fans justify their extra cost.

The back engine position shows its oddest weakness in mid-winter when snow has fallen and then turns into slush. This build-up in all the chassis nooks and crannies as the bus runs there to form a blanket around sundry pipe runs, only this blanket cools not warms.

The air brake system always contains some moisture which is thus encouraged to freeze and the first sign that anything is amiss will be the sudden failure of the air door gear, which incidentally continues despite improved drain valves.

A complete system shut down can follow when drive will be lost and so the resulting casualty has to be towed home, not that any great effort to rectify the situation will be necessary. Simply stand the bus over a nicely warmed pit and return in an hour or so when mobility in all departments will be restored, and it follows from this that with a forward engine there must always be sufficient heat wafting back to prevent annoyance of this sort from developing. One can add antifreeze but the effect is only temporary, so topping up becomes both frequent and at a quart and 1 quart a refill somewhat expensive.

If winter cools the underspace excessively the situation under the bonnet in summer must be vastly different, for short compressor life (it has of course a lot more to do in any event now that it also provides power for door, wiper, and gearbox operation) and a considerable build-up of carbon in the pipes adjacent to this unit have led to the adoption of water cooled heads and so still more water connections are called for, whilst completely jacketed units can now be obtained on special order.

This leads us naturally to the brakes and these too have their moments. The assemblies are well shrouded by deep wheel arches, and can become very hot. If automatic brake adjustors are fitted one can find that they will follow the surface of the ever-expanding drum until the work load eases and then sticking brakes are the order of the day. Various modifications have been tried to lay this annoyance to rest but in extreme cases a return to manual adjustment would appear to be the only answer.

Another hot spot is around the fluid flywheel. These were a troublesome device in earlier front-engined days until the bellows gland came into general use when shaft leakage was almost entirely eliminated. Now we are back in the development stage again and fully charged couplings are being tried, but their use currently is minimal and so a close watch on flywheel oil level has to be maintained.

Behind the flywheel is the gearbox and this certainly can receive a hammering although one must in all fairness say that some driving methods do nothing to help. Not very long ago I boarded a rear-engined vehicle one evening and had barely put my head in the door before my nostrils were assailed by the stench of very hot oil. The bus was on a one-man service, and my companion and I had hardly dropped our fares in the coin box when we were rocketed up the main road. The driver, a pleasant fellow, treated his passengers with courtesy and respect, attributes that did not extend alas to the bus. He kept his foot well down on the accelerator as he literally threw the gear lever from second to third and then into top, a process that was repeated almost without exception at every subsequent stop and also on the odd occasion when he elected to change down, until even the most unmechanically-minded passenger must have become aware of the cry for help that was coming from that gearbox.

Certain action followed but this is not the place to discuss whether the fault lay in lack of driver conscientiousness or of driver training. What is certain though is that had the process continued unchecked several hundred pounds worth of repair work would have become necessary within an hour or two.

Invariably the first sign of gearbox trouble comes

when the second gear drive fails and an initial examination will reveal that the friction band has worn down, but subsequent stripping usually reveals sundry other defects all brought about by component overheating. Older members of the fraternity faced with this type of thing will sadly compare the life returned by these rear-mounted boxes with that given by the old mid-frame located spring-loaded preselector units, but this is where the local factor can often come into the picture, otherwise why can one undertaking be deep in transmission troubles whilst another only a few miles away with jointly-worked services, the same type of vehicle, and apparently identical operating conditions averages around 100,000 miles per band renewal.

Mileage brings one to the engine and fortunately the well-tried Leyland 0.600 (later the 0680 engine) or the Gardner 6LX came to be fitted as standard in most vehicles of the type being reviewed here. They stand up to hard work surprisingly well and to prove the point I pulled one card out of a bus record file intending to set down what I read there. There was little to repeat just:

> Entered service September 1972
> Mileage to date 220,000
> Lub oil consumption first 2,500mpg
> last 910mpg
> Work done apart from the routine change of filters, injectors, and one repaired fuel lift pump . . . precisely nil.

I came to the conclusion that this might be exceptional so I looked over the other seven that form the rest of that particular batch. Two had had to have cylinder blocks changed due to partial seizure resulting from an undetected water hose failure, but apart from these the pattern was just the same and so we can confidently expect to see about 400,000 on the clock before a major overhaul will be necessary.

This optimistic forecast, though, must be qualified for some improvements have been made to the ventilation of the bonnet space since their first arrival by modifying the engine bay side panels so as to bring them up to more modern standards, but more ventilation can mean more dust coming into the area where it mixes with various oil vapours to build up into a greasy mass.

To some extent contamination can be reduced by providing dust shields, but the best solution is to indulge in a periodic steam cleaning exercise and this is always appreciated by the mechanics who are thus provided with better working conditions. Some of this oil vapour, however, will seep out from the bonnet lid joint and deposit itself along the rear fixed panelling so some appropriate night cleaner instructions are also often called for.

Other back end troubles have come from defective engine mounting cones which softened sufficiently to allow the metal of the mounting brackets to come into direct contact with the metal of the engine carrier foot (prompt action is always necessary here if further damage is to be avoided), gearbox input shaft failures, crankshaft flange leaks, insufficiently robust fan

Above right: Ingenious design. A Daimler Fleetline concentric shaft gearbox. Power goes in via the forked coupling, back to the front gearcase and via a train to the circular propeller shaft coupling flange. Later Fleetlines now have cast iron instead of alloy castings as originally used.

Centre right: Gardner power unit 1972 style. A 10.4litre 150bhp unit with alternator and water cooled compressor, looks rather different to its 4L2 predecessor but the low fuel consumption and high mileage traditions continue as strong as ever.

Below right: A modern Fleetline chassis. The reversed camber leaf springs, box-sectioned rear wheel arches, centre chassis pipe pins, substantial outrigger brackets and many other components can be clearly seen on this excellent photograph taken in the Radford Works yard.

Below: Prototype Fleetline 7000 HP had a Metro-Cammell body and a Daimler CVD6 engine. Finished in Birmingham Corporation colours it made many demonstration excursions in the early 1960s.

brackets or radiator mountings, leaking flexible exhaust pipe sections, and on very rare occasions loose fluid flywheels. Incidentally a good deal of valuable work has been done of late on exhaust systems and as a result use is being made of stainless steel in original manufacture.

As a general rule the rest of the chassis has been free from trouble. Rear axles are complicated especially where double reduction gearing is featured, but premature failures apart from odd half shaft shearings are never a subject for conversing engineers to get their teeth into.

Steering also seldom figures on the drivers' defects sheets but it is noticeable that quite a proportion of new 33ft long specifications call for the incorporation of some form of power assistance to ease the work load on the driver and particularly so where the buses are again intended for one man work.

There is though an interesting point involved here. Our first rear-engined double-deckers were built to a length of 30ft and, bearing in mind the mileage they have run up, no one has any reason to be dissatisfied with their performance, but all carried conductors.

One-man operation was restricted to single-deckers, but the various underfloor-engined buses used on this work suffered greatly when put into the heaviest routes and so an experiment was made with a small number of rear-engined saloons. These were built up to a length of 32ft, had 45 seats, the last two of which were positioned over the top of the engine, a two step front entrance, and an unladen weight of around 8½tons. Everything else was standard with their double-deck counterparts which were about 10cwt heavier, but it would appear from experience to date that the lack of a conductor is offset by this lightness factor for their service record has been outstanding. Their biggest fault is much reduced manoeuvrability which stems from the extra 2ft 3in the 18ft 6in wheelbase, but when similar chassis came to carry maximum length double-deck bodies which put up unladen weight by a ton or so mechanical problems increased out of all proportion, even before they were used on a one-man basis.

Brakes, gearboxes and engine life were the biggest sufferers following the disappearance of the second man, but this is really nothing new as we went through it all before when the regulations were amended a decade or so ago to allow forward engined buses to 'grow up' from 27ft to 30ft, or prior to that when earlier forward control single-deckers were adapted for omo duties.

The reader may think from all this that the rear-engined double-decker is a complete flop but nothing is further from the truth, although I must digress and mention the defect I never did diagnose. Only a few

Above: Bus No51 in the fleet of Great Yarmouth Corporation is based on chassis No60184 and was first used in service on 8 June 1963. Judging from the lack of varnish on the panels in front of the rear wheels it has recently suffered an 'inside wheelbase hook up' of the sort mentioned in the text.

days before I wrote this part of the book (May 1972) I decided to spend an evening bus riding in 'foreign parts'. The rear-engined machine I came to board half way through my circuitous journey was fairly new and almost empty so I took a seat at the front of the top deck.

We set off from a certain bus station quietly enough on an intertown route and until the suburbs were reached speed was kept at a sober pace. Just once was the 30 restriction touched when a I felt a peculiar motion but I put this down to the rather indifferent road surface. The country section was surprisingly busy. We stopped at every stop but then we reached a city limit and the start of both a new two-lane highway with a continual descent and a limited stop section. The driver who had lost a little time did what anyone else would have done and stepped on the gas when that bus began to gallop.

The front seat rose and fell in a series of sharp and rapid jerks and at around 35mph the intensity had to be experienced to be believed. Needless to say the rest of the equippage followed suit so by the time I finally alighted my system was so shaken that I positively embraced the elderly and spartenly-bodied Regent V — never one of my previous favourites — that took me on the next stage of my journey. As I was a stranger in a strange land I was not in a position to investigate the fault, but in over four decades of bus travel I have never before met the like and as a result I would have been only too pleased to have had the chance to probe the cause fully.

The fault with the rear-engined bus, if fault it is, comes from the inescapable fact that no matter how good designers are they can never cater for the inevitable weaknesses that only prolonged periods of service under widely varying conditions will reveal, and I cannot think of any buses, including the Tilling Stevens Express or the Bristol to mention two of the best of their day, that have not needed some development before they came to achieve wide spread acceptance, but these were of a relatively simple form.

The Atlantean was designed to carry a high number of seated passengers in modest box dimensions, give a

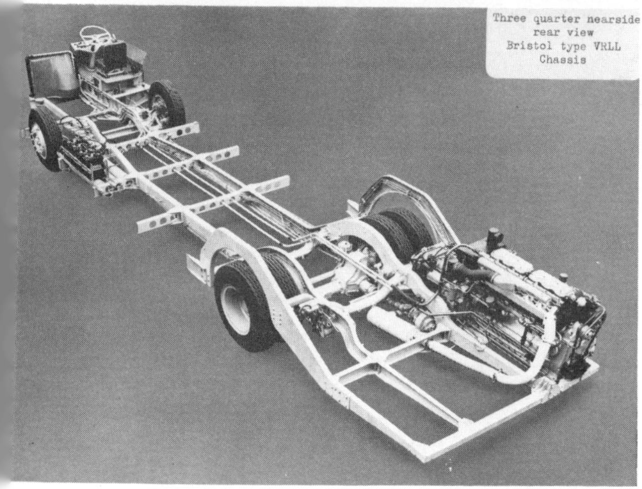

Above: Rear-engined single-decker. Mr Mayes the recently retired general manager of the Darlington undertaking, nearest the camera, surveys a new acquisition. Even though this bus can expect to have a long and successful career the easily accessible towing eyes represent a most sensible provision — engineers applaud.

Left: Different approach. The Bristol VRL displays a different approach by having an inline engine and a front radiator. The latter feature is also incorporated in the companion VRT model that has a transverse power unit.

low overall height, a low loading entrance that could be controlled by the drive, a good standard of ride, and by putting the entrance under the direct control of the driver reduce or totally eliminate platform accidents. It — and let us be fair — its imitators have done all this and more but such considerations meant that the traditional engine position could no longer be maintained. Some complexities had therefore to be included in a design which was intended to be 30ft long. At the operators' insistence it was stretched to 33ft but for production and cost reasons the same basic running units had to be employed. Then again at the operators' behest its use spread into the one-man field, and note here how I have referred at some length to the effect this can have on maintenance problems.

These will be overcome without doubt but perhaps we are currently expecting too much from a concept which is scarcely a decade old and which had these greater demands imposed upon it during that period.

I doubt if anyone would really want to contemplate a return to the open platform crash gearbox, vacuum braked machine on which most of the present generation of senior engineers, myself included, cut their teeth, but one of the fascinations of the job is that both manufacturers and the industry are always trying to do better and never failing to display a good deal of initiative in the process.

At this point it is pertinent to point out that I have in this chapter confined my remarks in the main to the older versions of the Leyland Atlantean and Daimler Fleetline machines even though both have been the subject of a whole series of modifications to improve their service availability.

These buses, too, utilise one version or other of the well tried Wilson preselective gearbox in a semi-automatic form but, of course, there are other types of buse and more recent designs of transmission unit now on the market ranging from the unique front engined Ailsa, through the more traditionally orientated Dennis Dominator, or the Foden of similar mien, to the sophisticated Metropolitans, Metrobuses or Titans, most of which come complete with fully automatic transmission and retarders.

Our service experience to date is such that it is almost impossible to comment factually upon the sort of performance they will return in the days to come, but one thing is certain ... even with these magnificent machines, we shall not have left 'all our troubles behind' and so the task of maintenance engineer is going to be just as essential and even more fascinating than it ever was. It is truly a wonderful trade.

Postscript

The ideal bus would be all things to all men —

The manufacturer wishes to see a vehicle which is easy to build from a production point of view and will in the end provide a reasonable profit margin. The operator wants a competitive price and a machine that will give an adequate return on the capital expenditure over a long number of years. His engineer wants something that will work day after day with the minimum of maintenance, whilst the other important official, the traffic manager, is looking for a vehicle that will carry a good load with a minimum crew requirement. The crew members, who will man the bus for up to eight hours, do want reasonable working conditions together with adequate performance as an absolute minimum and something well over that level if at all possible. Last, but by no means least, the passenger, without whom there would be no bus service anyway, is happy when easy entrances and exits are provided together with a high standard of comfort, a factor which involves seats, suspension, low noise levels and those two conflicting desirabilities of very hot heating and cool fresh air ventilation.

Consequently any design must be a compromise between these varying criteria and as a result we are involved in a continuous process of development in pursuit of the attainment of this ideal.

It is this development programme which has been responsible for every one of the buses mentioned in these pages, but a careful reader will have noted that almost without exception every thing new produces some servicing problems, oft times of a quite unexpected nature. It will also have been noted that these difficulties can, and do, vary surprisingly from place to place and that invariably the manufacturers follow up service complaints with a commendable despatch.

This all means that a modern bus, despite certain apparent failings, is always a good deal better than is predecessors. To take one example: the Tilling Stevens Express had a wonderful reputation in its day, but it could never stand up to modern traffic requirements and, if it could, then crew costing would make its operation a most uneconomical business.

Here praise should be given to those unsung heroes, the oil technologists, the metallurgists and other backroom boys who from time to time achieve some significant breakthrough.

In the end, though, it is the garage staffs who keep the wheels turning.

Their work can be hard and dirty and even involve some anxious moments, but it also has its lighter side. Fortunately it is this aspect of the job which continues to remain in one's memory, and perhaps it is for this reason that few who enter the engineering side of the passenger transport industry are ever heard to express regret about their chosen profession. Almost to a man they agree that it is all a most fascinating business and long may it so remain.